MW01132292

PRAISE FOR

NAVIGATE THE CLIMB

"I have known Maria for over twenty years as her mentor and friend. Rarely have I met someone who is in such command of her life and is as resilient as Maria. Her hard-won lessons in her professional and personal life are a must-read guidebook as you navigate the climb. It will strengthen your journey."

—Jane S. Goldner, PhD
Author of *Women Driven to Success: You Can Have It YOUR All*

"Major General (retired) Maria Britt's whole life has been about shattering glass ceilings and beating long odds by following her True North. In *Navigate the Climb*, she draws from the lessons of her own experience to create an indispensable guide to discovering and pursuing your own True North."

—William B. Caldwell IV
Lieutenant General (U.S. Army, Retired)
President, Georgia Military College

"Maria is a born trailblazer with the grit and class to lead others into the future. She is a gifted keynote speaker and engaging leader who brings forth her tenacity in a very genuine and relatable way. She has inspired and sparked action in male and female leaders across many industries and demographics. Her book is a must-read!"

—Jennifer H. Kozel
Senior Manager Talent Acquisition, The Home Depot

"The next generation of women leaders can thank Maria Britt for her straight-up advice and clear insights into navigating both personal and professional leadership success. Her recounting of the challenges of being 'the first' as she broke the glass ceiling on multiple levels without women role models makes for a compelling read and road map. Her book is a powerful testimony to striving and thriving in a male-dominated environment. Great job on paying it forward."

—Jeffery Tobias Halter
President, YWomen – Corporate Gender Consulting

"A great read for all leaders and aspiring leaders who seek to be the best in both their personal and professional lives. Major General (retired) Maria Britt's *Navigate the Climb: Leadership for Life's Journey* stands out among leadership books. She puts it all out there, from challenges and struggles in her personal life to searching for her purpose while changing careers. Britt offers her unique and insightful lessons, practical advice, and tools. For the business executive, as well as first-time civilian or military leaders, you will take away practical lessons to apply, derived from raising three successful children to breaking glass ceilings in rising to be the first female general officer in the Georgia National Guard."

—P. K. (Ken) Keen, Lieutenant General (U.S. Army, Retired)
Associate Dean for Leadership Development,
Emory University Goizueta Business School

"Drawing on her vast personal knowledge of leadership challenges in the military, Major General (retired) Maria Britt gives practical advice on how to succeed in the business world. She uses humor and candor to deliver lessons you won't want to learn on your own. While most of us will never face the life-or-death decisions Maria did, we can learn from obstacles she overcame and opportunities she seized on her road to the top."

—Erin Wolf
Founding Director, Women's Leadership Center,
Kennesaw State University
Author of *Lessons from the Trenches*

"Focusing less on theory and more on the pragmatics of becoming an effective leader, Maria Britt's detailed philosophy provides the reader with a rich tour de force of the attitudes and skills needed to become highly successful, regardless of the career. Written in a no-nonsense, accessible style, *Navigate the Climb: Leadership for Life's Journey* provides a rare description of how to balance the good and bad of organizational life, reflecting on lessons learned and demonstrating a clarity self-grounded in moral courage. This book should serve as required reading for new leaders and those who mentor new leaders."

—Randy C. Hinds, PhD
Colonel (U.S. Army, Retired)

NAVIGATE THE CLIMB

NAVIGATE THE CLIMB

Leadership for Life's Journey

Maria L. Britt
Major General (U.S. Army, Retired)

BOOKLOGIX'

Alpharetta, GA

ISBN: 978-1-61005-949-7 – Paperback
eISBN: 978-1-61005-950-3 – ePub
eISBN: 978-1-61005-951-0 – mobi

Library of Congress Control Number: 2019903933

10 9 8 7 6 5 4 3 2   070819

Printed in the United States of America

♾This paper meets the requirements of ANSI/NISO Z39.48-1992 (Permanence of Paper)

To my daughters,
Ava, Chelsea, and Joy.
You inspired me to write this book.

To my parents,
Anthony and Dolores Corsini.
Thank you for always believing in me.

Anyone can steer the ship, but it takes a leader to chart the course.

—John Maxwell

CONTENTS

INTRODUCTION

I'm not supposed to cry. I'm not supposed to cry . . .

But as they began to shut the coffin lid, I couldn't help myself. The tears came. The emotions that I had been fighting to hide were there as I shared the grief of the family beside me over the tragic loss of a young soldier whom I had helped train. I cried alongside his loved ones over a life lost too soon. Seeing the pain his mother and father were going through, I struggled to maintain my composure.

This is not what a leader should do. Right?

I was taught that as a leader, I should control my emotions, remain poised and calm—but as a woman, crying is a natural reaction. It was hard to fight that compassionate side of myself, the side that compelled me to stay with the soldier's body, never leaving his side the entire time. It was a tragic accident—mistakenly shot by his best friend in his living room as they were reenacting that week's training. A bullet wasn't supposed to be in the chamber. They were experienced marksmen as military police soldiers and SWAT team members. Just weeks earlier for a Father's Day visit, his dad had warned his son to be more careful with the weapons.

I had just been reassigned, but felt it my duty to escort this young soldier from Georgia back home to Seattle. I had flown across the country, ridden to the funeral home, and stayed for the wake and viewing, refusing to eat and only being away long enough to use the restroom. I felt compelled to be there, to watch over him on his final journey on Earth. As a mother, I couldn't help but to internalize the pain of his own grieving mother. Hours earlier, I had scrambled to clean the soldier's shirt after discovering he had aspirated on his chest during the airplane cargo-bay transport. I wouldn't allow his family to see him that way. He was still my soldier.

In my life I have constantly felt caught in this trap of wanting to be genuine and "be myself," while at the same time portraying a strong leader who is acting more like a man—all to be accepted by the people I lead. We're taught to control our responses as leaders, and that can be difficult. The very last thing you want to do is cry; they're expecting that. How many women have been misjudged in the professional environment because they were caught shedding tears? Crying causes a person, man or woman, to somehow be viewed as "weak" by their peers.

I realized that to continue on my journey of paving the way for other female leaders, I would need to get to that point where I could better compartmentalize my emotions, but still be authentic. Compassion and leadership can often be like oil and water. Finding the right combination while still being myself was a constant struggle for me as I navigated my climb toward the top.

What does it really mean to be a leader? You don't have to be a CEO, politician, or a general in the military to be considered a leader. Teachers, for instance, lead the children in their classroom. Another example, parents, are leaders of their children. It's incredible how many people do not realize that the principles of leadership are similar to those of being a good parent.

The leader guides the team members—be they children, students, or staff—toward achieving a greater mission or vision. A leader is focused on the "big picture," but isn't just telling other people what to do all day. A good leader is not feared, but respected. A good leader inspires others around them to feel they are part of the cause and doing something with purpose, rather than making them feel that they are trapped in a dead-end job. Many are eager to move up into a leadership role without truly understanding the leader's role in their organization. Or, they may already see themselves as a leader because they are a manager or a boss of some kind. Don't confuse being in a leadership position with being a leader.

Each of us can be a leader in our own environment, should we choose to be. Although I did not know when I was a child that I would become the first woman in the 273-year history of the Georgia Army National Guard to make the rank of general officer, command eleven thousand soldiers as the major general, and be named one of the top ten most powerful women in Georgia, I *did* know I was destined for leadership. My leadership skills were honed over my adult life and came to fruition as I stepped up for the greatest challenge of my career: serving as commanding general of the Georgia Army National Guard. My mission to train, equip, and ensure the readiness of the thousands of Guardsmen under my command became my passion. Every decision I made was driven by a need to support the mission and the vision. My purpose was to serve the greater good, and to harness the power of the team that would ultimately achieve the mission.

Many people are destined for leadership, but they must first get past the issues holding them back. They must make the right decisions, choose the right path, and always set a good example. They have to be willing to take risks. I have never stuck to the script. Taking chances to chart your own course can be painful, but it pays off. I have had periods of great stress in my life, but also great success. My time in the service ended with being awarded the Distinguished Service Medal—the second-highest medal the U.S. Army bestows, and the same medal given to the likes of Eisenhower, Patton, and MacArthur, my dad's childhood heroes. The award came shortly after a very difficult period, and provided a much-needed recognition of my tireless devotion to the military and the soldiers' families, especially those who had lost loved ones. I never would have accomplished what I have thus far in my life if I hadn't exceeded the limits of my bosses' expectations, always doing what was best for the organization I was serving.

Early on in my career I challenged myself to break the glass ceiling for women coming up in the ranks behind me. However, I have found through years of mentoring and providing leadership training that there are many principles and practices I developed that can help both sexes. Whether male or female, many of the issues future leaders face today are very much the same. There will be both men and women in positions of power above you who will make you feel uncomfortable. I have faced my fair share of successes and challenges, and can honestly say that the climb to the top is never an easy one, regardless of how far up the mountain you begin.

In the upcoming chapters I will share methods to develop yourself as a leader that you can adopt for your own use, whether or not you have yet entered a leadership role in your life. You will learn that leadership starts within yourself. If you cannot lead yourself, you surely won't be able to lead others.

I will share with you my traits of an effective leader, so that you can work on developing your own leadership style. Being a good leader doesn't mean being skilled at bossing others around—there's much more to it than that. Moreover, adopting strategic leadership traits is not something that happens overnight. You must be prepared to take a long, hard look at yourself from the inside out, and make changes in your attitude, actions, and overall mental state.

By sharing both the professional and personal adversity I have faced and overcome, it is my hope that you will feel inspired in your own leadership journey.

The secret of getting ahead is getting started.
—Mark Twain

I

FINDING YOUR INNER COMPASS

What's Driving You?

W hat do you want out of life? What are you living for? What were you put on this earth to do? And finally, when was the last time you really sat back and thought about it? We get so wrapped up in the day-to-day of our lives that we often don't take time to think about the larger picture. Yet it's critical in your development as a leader to identify your purpose.

Every effective leader moves in the direction of a destination. Not a literal destination, but a goal or a purpose—the True North. The reference comes from the use of a compass, and finding your way back by aiming your compass at "true north." True North is a way to stay focused on your journey. Once you know what you are working toward, every action you take and every decision you make should keep that True North in mind. It doesn't have to be profession oriented; it just has to be what you want to achieve the most. For me, that is servant leadership—leading because you want to accomplish things for others. I wanted to pave the way, making the path easier for the women who came after me in the military and the boardroom. In short, this is what I am constantly working toward—the greater good—having an impact on something bigger than myself, inspiring others, and helping to shape the next generation of leaders.

Staying focused on my True North has not been easy. Along my journey in life I have hit many speed bumps and potholes. But I dusted myself off, licked my wounds, and persevered by recalibrating my True North—my desire to be a servant leader.

"Pick Something Else"

I was born into an Italian-Catholic family, and faith was a big part of our lives. I decided as a child that I was going to be a priest when I grew up. I had a deep respect and devotion for those who served the Lord and led a parish. My father had told me that I could be whatever I wanted to be, and I took him literally. One day I performed a mass with my four cousins, brother, and sister. I had the mass pretty much memorized, and we were going through it, kneeling, sitting . . . until my mother walked by and asked me what we were doing.

"I'm the priest, Mom," I answered.

She looked at me and said, "You can't be a priest in the Catholic Church. You're a girl. You need to pick something else." It was a defining moment for me, to be told by my mother that I couldn't do something that I believed in after hearing my father assure me I could be anything I wanted.

Still wanting to serve, I set my sights on becoming a nun. I respected, admired, and to some extent as a good Catholic girl, feared them. As I got older there were times when I questioned the career choice, but never the motive behind it. In fourth grade, after a humiliating incident with a nun and a paddle in front of my class, I wondered, *How could they do this to me?* Nuns were women of the cloth, following Christ's example of not judging and always forgiving. Being paddled destroyed the saintly attributes I had ascribed to them. But I was still determined to be in a profession where I could serve others—a higher calling.

Fortunately, in 1976 Congress authorized women to attend military-service academies. I was just entering high school, and my father sat down with me and explained that the military could be another way for me to become a servant leader. He also pointed out to me that life as a nun would prohibit me from experiencing certain things, such as being a wife or mother. So my father and I began researching West Point. I planned my entire high school experience around the goal of attending West Point to become the best leader possible. I was driven, academically focused, and athletic. Although their siblings had served, my parents had no previous military experience, and I wasn't even sure I wanted to be a military officer, but I made up my mind.

When I was accepted, I felt confident that even though it was a male-dominated profession, I could make a difference. Yet I wasn't even thinking about the reality of being a woman in G.I. Joe's world. Was I about to get a wake-up call.

A History of Gender Bias

There is a long history of gender bias in mankind's story, and not just in obvious places such as the military. Although in many ways society has come a long way in the progress of equality between the sexes, there is still a long road ahead. Wage gaps, maternity leave, and childcare are major issues in today's professional landscape, among other gender-equality topics. In a variety of workplaces women are treated in a different manner than their male counterparts, given different dress codes and standards of appearance, passed over for promotions or certain positions . . . the list goes on and on.

While women make up about half of the workforce in America today,[1] there is a disappointing gap when it comes to leadership positions: the higher the level of power, the fewer the percentages of women. Women hold around 4 percent of CEO positions in America's companies on the Fortune 500 list.[2] The number of CFOs isn't much better, at under 15 percent.[3] The lack of female leadership is likely in part because of negative perceptions of female leaders. In the past, studies have demonstrated that even when female leaders exhibit the same qualities as their male counterparts, they are misconstrued. For example, when women assert themselves, it can be perceived by employees as being controlling or domineering; when males demonstrate the same behavior, it is perceived as being bold and decisive.

Although many strides have been made since I entered West Point, the military is known for a history of bias against women. Deborah Sampson, the first woman ever recorded in U.S. history to fight on the battlefield for our country, hid the fact that she was female altogether.[4] In order to fight for our country during a time when women were not allowed in the military, Deborah quit her job as a schoolteacher, cut her hair, bound her chest, and called herself Robert Shurtliff. In 1782, Deborah enlisted as a Continental soldier. She was tough as nails. In one battle, redcoat soldiers shot Deborah in the leg. The blast knocked her off her horse and injured her severely, filling her calf with pellets. Legend has it that Deborah stood up, walked off, and without any anesthesia, used a penknife to dig the pellets out on her own. She couldn't take her chances of a medic discovering her secret. So she did what she had to do.

A doctor eventually discovered Deborah's secret. But instead of reporting her, the doctor was so impressed with Deborah's passion for service that he kept her gender a secret. It wasn't until after the war ended in 1783 that the doctor revealed Deborah's identity to General John Paterson. Deborah was summoned to West Point, New York, where she was given an honorable discharge. Deborah's True North was to serve her country, and she took great risks to move her life toward that purpose.

You may not have to go to the extremes that Deborah Sampson did to reach your True North, but whether you are male or female, there will always be obstacles in your way. There will be those who, for whatever reason, will try to hold you back professionally, and perhaps personally, as well.

Breaking the Glass Ceiling at West Point

I entered West Point in 1979 as a member of the fourth class integrated with women. Much of the school was still adjusting to the idea of women being at the academy. On the first day of my academic year, my roommate, Sharon, and I were getting our dorm ready, and we heard a loud knock on the door. We knew it was our squad leader; we told him to enter. He kicked the door in—a big guy with a scar on his shaved head, West Point shorts, and a T-shirt. We were scared to death, and he took one look at the two of us and sputtered, "Fuck! Women . . ." Since the nameplates on the doors only had last names, he didn't know that he had two female cadets for the year. We were prejudged before we even had the chance to show what we were made of. I knew then that it was going to be a tough year. My roommate and I worked extra hard at everything, and we earned his respect in time. He went from dismissive and angry to actually warding off upper-class cadets when we were receiving more than our fair share of "one-on-one counseling."

Unfortunately, many of the difficulties I faced in my time at West Point weren't with leadership or instructors, but with other cadets, and even other women. On Reception Day, or R Day, everyone gets a haircut: men's heads are shaved and women's hair is cut. I had gotten my hair cut before leaving home, and my cut had been okayed on the first day. But a week or two later, one senior female cadet decided she had a problem with my hair, and would grab it and tell me I needed to "do something with this hair." I wanted to explain that I had been told my hair was fine, but there was no talking back allowed. It was an interesting time, because there were now three classes of women that had come before mine. A few of them wanted to make sure that we had it as bad as they did.

I was terrified of this woman, and I knew she would come back at me again if I didn't do something. So I got a pair of scissors and cut my own hair. The results were not pretty. I butchered my hair. This, of course, caused me to get in trouble with my squad leader, because now my hair was actually too short! The barber couldn't do anything with it, and so I had to keep my service hat on at all times when I was outside the cadets' area. The academy brought me before a council to determine if I should be punished, which luckily I was not. At the time I didn't understand the implications of what I had done to myself in the larger scheme of things. West Point was under a great deal of pressure for the way they were integrating women. If someone had gotten a photo of me with my butchered hair, it could have been spun to make the academy look bad.

People warned me the other cadets would test and push newcomers, that it was a weeding-out process. But when you are the one actually being harassed, it doesn't feel like a game; it feels personal. One night I was walking briskly with my shoulder up against the wall, doing errands, when a sophomore got in my face, using slurs about me being a woman and saying something about me being ditzy. I could feel the disdain in his voice and see the disgust in his eyes. I was in the wrong place at the wrong time, as he was obviously having a bad day. He finally said, "You're nothing but a space cadet."

All of a sudden, I snapped. I let him get to me. I had made it through the whole summer of Beast Barracks (the equivalent of basic training in the Army), yet this guy found a chink in my armor. I tried to choke back my tears, but couldn't. I started crying out of both anger at myself and hatred for his ugliness. His lack of respect for me made me disrespect him.

It made me doubt if this was what I wanted to do. If this was an example of leadership, then it wasn't for me. Finally, I pulled myself together, knowing that tomorrow would be another day. I think he may have realized he went too far, because the next day he approached me and offered to help me with a computer-science course. I knew that even if I was failing the course I could never accept his help. I had lost all respect for him, and couldn't fathom the thought of him contributing to my success. He departed West Point after his sophomore year, just before you're committed to a five-year obligation. I knew he wasn't at West Point to prepare to serve his country; he was in it for himself.

The incident was a turning point for me. I realized two important lessons. First, I had just witnessed a negative leadership style that I would never embrace or tolerate in my organization. Second, I realized he was playing a mental game, and I had let him win. Never again would I let someone get to me like that.

Stay in the Fight

There were many naysayers anxious to derail me from taking steps to reach my True North. I learned as time went on that I couldn't take it personally. Many felt that women should not be at West Point, and would try to take steps to run women out of the academy. I remember one tactical officer who would take the platoon out on runs and try to make me and my roommate, Jane, look bad. She and I were squad leaders in the platoon, and both runners, fortunately. He would pick up the pace and go longer and longer. We were able to keep up, so all he was doing was causing all the males to drop out, because Jane and I would never quit. Years later when I was at Fort McPherson as a captain, he came up to me and asked if I remembered him. Of course I did. Then, he actually apologized for his actions. He said that he had firmly believed that women didn't belong at the academy at that time, though Jane and I had proved him wrong and helped him to better respect women. Now that he had served in the Army for some time, he understood the importance of having women in the ranks, and was sorry for what he had done. I was in total shock, but accepted his apology. I walked away after a crisp salute, realizing that you can't take on the whole world, but you can change it one person at a time.

I did come close to leaving West Point, but just one time. Before I had started my new cadet boot camp, my dad told me that if I ever changed my mind, all I had to do was call and he'd come get me and take me home. I went so far as to call him one night, asking him to pick me up the next day. Without hesitation, he replied, "I'll be there tomorrow to get you." I spent a long night questioning myself. Was I simply not tough enough to handle the military? Would taking another career path make me happier, or would I feel like I was losing out on what I really wanted? I came to the realization that my loss of self-confidence had resulted from the constant barrage of negativity imposed by my superiors.

That night, I decided that this was not about me; it was about women. I was the victim of stereotyping, and if I wanted to overcome those stereotypes, I would have to work harder and smarter. I refocused my compass once again on my True North—my desire for a life of servant leadership, and my driving force to make the way easier for the women coming after me. I realized then and still believe today that you can't influence an outcome if you don't stay in the fight.

I called my dad back the next morning to tell him I was staying. There was silence on the line, and then he exclaimed, "I knew you'd change your mind!"

Something Was Missing

My time at West Point was very busy and very regimented. Nearly every minute of every day was scheduled, except Sunday, which we had as a free day. While growing up, my family had gone to church every Sunday. I wanted to be a priest, then a nun, and so religion was very important to me, but somehow in all the craziness of my first year at West Point I had gotten lazy when it came to nurturing my soul. I remember that I felt a little depressed, homesick, lonely . . . but it was more than that. I had an empty feeling, like something was missing. After a while, and after first trying to fill the void with Häagen-Dazs ice cream, I figured out what the problem might be. I decided to test my theory, and went to the Catholic chapel on post.

It was smaller than St. Mary's in Gloversville, the church I grew up attending, but cozy. The church was empty as I entered late that day, and as I walked in, the musty incense smell of the chapel just hit me. Taking a few more steps, I noted a ray of sun shining through the stained glass, lighting up the chapel. I knelt down at a pew and started praying, and was suddenly overwhelmed with emotion. I broke down crying and realized that what I had been missing was my faith. I had turned away from the Lord and was trying to control everything in my life. I was putting so much focus into my activities at West Point that I had lost a sense of myself in the process, and had let go of the very thing that had helped keep me focused and grounded throughout my youth.

I had become a bit angry; the Lord was allowing me to be put through these trials and difficulties at West Point. I wanted someone to blame, and isn't that what humans do, blame God? Yet in that moment, I realized that I had no one to blame but myself. I had made the decision that had gotten me to this point in my life, a woman breaking ground in a man's world. From that day on, I promised that I would never turn away from the Lord again, no matter what happened in my life. Letting my faith back into my life revived me, and helped to get me through some very hard times then and ever since. My faith will always be a big part of who I am, and a big part of what keeps me aimed in the direction of my True North.

Like me, you may get sidetracked or deviate from practices that are important to you from time to time. It's easy to get caught up in the busyness of life. As a leader, you need to be able to identify when you feel yourself slipping and use your internal compass to set yourself back on course.

Support System

When you're trying to break down barriers, you really need to have people who believe in you on your "team" as you take on challenges. When you face the inevitable series of challenges that may cause you to want to give up your fight, you will need a support system to help give you strength. Luckily, I have been blessed with a supportive family who did not question my decisions, and was there for me to lean on when I needed extra support. My parents were both very understanding of the challenges that were ahead for me and my sister as women, and they made sure to prepare us from a young age. My mom and dad had seen the struggles of their parents, who had emigrated from Italy speaking very little English. My dad had sisters who did not have the opportunity to go to college and had to stay in bad marriages because they could not support themselves. He didn't want his daughters to face the same kinds of issues later in life. He drilled into me early on that I needed to go into math or science, especially as a woman, because I was "already behind." He knew that I would be paid less for my work than a man in the same position, so he encouraged me to go into science, math, and engineering fields because they offered better earning potential.

My mom was ahead of her time, attending college at Pratt Institute of Design in New York City, and later, at the urging of my dad, getting her teaching certificate in art education. In addition to stressing the importance of an education, my father wanted my sister and I to always be able to support ourselves, along with any future children.

My father set a high standard for himself as well. Married in 1959, he enrolled in Albany State University in 1961, earning both a bachelor's and a master's in American studies by 1965, all while having three children, commuting forty miles each way to college during the day, and running a business at night. He went on to teach students for almost thirty years. Looking back, I realize that my father was really ahead of his time in his views of women and their role impacting society. Little did I know how important this advice would be later in my life's journey.

When I began at West Point there wasn't a support system for women, and obviously none of the men knew what we were going through. I no longer had my family right there with me, nor a network of women to lean on. But I had one silent supporter that I will always be grateful for.

In freshman (or "plebe") year, cadets must take turns calling the minutes for each of the hallways in the mornings. We would stand against the wall calling out the minutes left until formation along with the uniform and menu for the day. It was during my calling-out minutes when I noticed our janitor, a short Italian man named Emmanuel, sometimes looking at me while sweeping. He noticed on my name tag that my last name, Corsini, was Italian, and so one day he asked me my first name. You're not supposed to speak while minutes are being called out, so I was afraid I'd get in trouble, but I didn't see anyone around, so I told him my name was Maria. He told me he had a daughter by the same name. He went back to his sweeping, then later came back and spoke to me more. This became a sort of routine every morning before formation.

When there are witnesses, bullies don't necessarily want to show their true colors. Emmanuel realized that if he stuck close to me while sweeping, they wouldn't haze me as much. He became my guardian angel. Every morning he would come out and sweep in our hallway somewhere around me, and it worked. If someone did start to bother me, he would start sweeping closer. We didn't talk, but we were forming this bond, and I knew what he was doing. One day he told me that if I ever needed anything, to ask him.

He came to my rescue later when my roommate threw a football to me in our room. I'm a runner, not a ball player—I followed my instincts and ducked. The football sailed past, broke the window, and rested in the gutter below. We looked out and saw it out on a stoop in the gutter with shards of broken glass. We were going to be in serious trouble. I realized that we needed help, and so I suggested to her that we try Emmanuel. I wrote a note, snuck downstairs to the janitors' sinks (where freshmen weren't allowed to go), and left a note for him. It said something like "Please help, we broke a window in our room, if there's anything you can do . . . our first inspection is at 1:00 p.m."

Later when we went back to our room after class, we realized that the window had been fixed. Emmanuel had gotten it done within the day and fixed the glass perfectly. You wouldn't have even known. I was very grateful. He kept both of us from getting demerits. I thanked him profusely, but quietly, the next morning.

Emmanuel used to tell me while sweeping around my feet, "Time pass'a fast. Don't you worry, time pass'a fast," he'd say.

"Emmanuel, it's not passing fast."

"Shh, time will pass'a fast."

He said it to me every day, and I've always kept that in mind. He could tell that I was dealing with an incredible amount of stress, and he wanted me to know that eventually it would be over. Over time, I came to believe that Emmanuel, a name that translates into "savior," was the answer to my prayers. I now know that time waits for no one; it just passes you by and tomorrow a new day will dawn.

Compass Check: What Is Your True North?

My True North of someday having a career in servant leadership was my driving force. From being told I couldn't be a priest and deciding to be a nun instead, to being hazed by both men and women cadets and officers, I faced many challenges in my early days. But my compass always pointed me back to my True North.

To reach *your* True North, you'll need to identify what will keep you heading in the right direction throughout your path in life. What makes you want to get out of bed every morning? What is your heartfelt purpose for living? Is it a career goal? Is it being a better parent to your children? With so many personal and professional obstacles in our way on a daily basis, it can be easy to stray from reaching our True North, but staying focused and soldiering on in the face of adversity is the key to your growth as a leader. Once you identify your True North, focus your compass in that direction and start moving.

If you know the enemy and know yourself, you
need not fear the result of a hundred battles.
—Sun Tzu, *The Art of War*

II

DISCOVER YOUR TRUE NORTH

A Personal Leadership Philosophy

Have you ever wondered how impactful leaders emerge in society or on the global stage? Leadership is a potential skill that very few are born with. Only rarely are people equipped to immediately start leading other people, personally or professionally. I have observed leaders around me for decades, and I have come to believe that those who lead successfully first learned how to lead *themselves*. You have to be prepared to take on challenges, make mistakes, and learn from those mistakes. You must be mentally prepared as you identify your mission and work tirelessly toward it. You must exude confidence in who you are and your abilities. How can you lead a team, let alone a company, if you cannot first "lead" yourself? It is necessary to become secure in who you are as a leader before you take on the task of leading others.

Many people see leaders, managers, or parents that they admire and assume those people were just "born that way." I wouldn't necessarily say that I was "born" a leader. I grew and developed into the leader, mentor, and parent that I am today. I grew up wanting to lead and to serve a greater good. It wasn't until my experience at West Point that I realized I needed to develop my skill set in leadership, but first I had to be comfortable in my own skin.

Years ago I discovered a secret: the application of leadership principles is actually the same in both your personal and professional life. As a parent, there are many skills needed in order to be effective. I need to be a good listener when my children are trying to express themselves to me. I have to listen carefully to each one of their sides to a story when they are fighting and look to me to help resolve the conflict. I often need to be patient with them as they make mistakes or bad decisions and slowly grow into adults. I expect them to tell the truth—the whole truth—to me at all times. When they behave badly or don't tell the truth, there are consequences. Although I am sometimes disappointed in their actions, I still love them.

These same characteristics apply in a professional environment as well. I need to be a good listener with my staff and my managers. I must listen carefully when there is debate in my team about a conflict or difficult issue that requires resolution. And, of course, I always expect my staff to tell me the truth. There will be consequences for poor performance, as well as rewards for superior performance. When someone on the team makes a mistake, I will be disappointed but expect them to learn from it. I will still respect the person while focusing on the resolution.

I was not a risk-taker when I was young. I was the teen who never got into trouble, was totally focused on my grades, and didn't deceive myself about what my limitations were. I was a self-proclaimed nerd and proud of it. Choosing to attend West Point was really the first risk I had taken. And in my time there, I confronted many risks and challenges that helped me not only see life in a new way, but develop skills and philosophies I still carry with me today.

The Courage to Jump

As part of my training at West Point, I was selected to attend the U.S. Army Jungle Warfare School in Panama. During the last training event, there were just three steps between me and the feat of becoming one of the first women in history to complete Jungle Warfare School. However, at the end of those steps was a hundred-foot drop into Limon Bay, Panama, followed by a difficult swim to an RB15 (rubber boat for fifteen people). *Just jump, Maria,* I thought. *Jump from the chopper, keep my weapon out of the water, and get on that raft.*

It was a windy day, and the Chinook struggled to stay steady. We were higher than we should have been for a free-fall jump, especially in rough weather, and the helicopter rocked wildly as I tried to steady my feet. I was wearing heavy equipment and carrying an M16 rifle for the amphibious-assault exercise that would follow the helocast jump. As I checked the security of my life vest and gear, I made eye contact with my battle buddy. He gave me a nod. Once we landed in the water, we'd immediately check on each other. I had his back, and I knew he had mine; we had practiced this exercise the day before. It only works when everyone jumps within seconds of the previous jumper.

As with life, the plan doesn't always get executed as it is practiced. The jump master didn't like something he saw on a jumper who was going ahead of me. He made immediate corrections to rectify the problem, but it only takes seconds to throw off the jumping sequence. I watched my battle buddy disappear below the tailgate—there one moment, gone the next.

When it was my turn, I gritted my teeth and stepped out. Jumping took all the courage I had. As I dropped toward the water, I didn't have time to think about how we were higher than we should have been. I didn't have time to think about keeping the rifle dry or locking my arms in position over my head. I didn't have time to think about how I was supposed to land at a forty-five-degree angle. I just jumped.

I slammed into the water at the wrong angle. The handgrip of my rifle smashed down on my face, breaking my nose in two places and knocking me out. When I came to, I was facedown and disoriented in the water with no battle buddy to check on me. I heard someone yell for a boat with a medic. Another classmate swam over and held my head out of the water while other hands lifted me into the rescue boat. I was still seeing stars when I landed, battered, in the bottom of the boat. Two U.S. Marines rushed to stop the bleeding with the only rags they could find. I could barely breathe through all the blood.

"You're bleeding all over my shorts!" one of the Marines barked at me. In my daze I thought, *Why would he wear white shorts to a jungle mission, anyway?*

Within a few minutes I heard more yelling, and the boat headed over to rescue another classmate who had been injured in the same way. His weapon came down on his face and ripped off his upper lip while knocking out his two front teeth. He was bleeding just as much as me.

We were both stitched up in a rudimentary veterinary clinic and showed the door. There was still another day to go at Fort Sherman before I was to fly back to upstate New York. My face swelled to a big black-and-blue blob, and my black eyes were swollen so tight I couldn't see. I had to put my hand on a classmate's shoulders to be guided around. Meanwhile, some of the cadre were trying to take pictures of me. My fellow West Pointers blocked me from the cameras, but someone managed to snap a picture of my disfigured face. I looked like a zombie.

A few months later, I got news from a friend of a friend who was a U.S. Army Ranger assigned at the Jungle Warfare School in Panama. In the cadre's lounge there was a company bulletin board, and on it, someone had posted the picture of my battered face. There was a caption underneath: *This is what happens when women come to this school.*

My fellow injured male cadet had looked as ghastly as I did, but his injury wasn't the headline of our exercise—mine was. There were some who took pride in the fact that I couldn't finish that exercise without getting injured. They were the same people who didn't give my male counterpart a hard time for also getting injured.

It was embarrassing and frustrating, but I didn't let it defeat me, even though it was unjust. I told myself that it wasn't done to hurt me personally; they didn't even know my name. They were just using me as a poster child to make a point. They felt women shouldn't be allowed to train alongside them, to serve the country in the same way as men. I knew that if I lowered myself to their level and came off the high ground, I'd get dirty, too. I didn't realize it then, but I was already shaping my leadership philosophy for life.

While you may make mistakes or be seen as "not good enough," your abilities won't always be overlooked if you work hard and lead well. My perseverance paid off in the end. When I entered West Point there were 120 women in a class of 1,400—less than 9 percent of the class. We ended with just 60 women in a class of 800—less than 8 percent—and I was one of them. Best of all, many women soldiers have come after me and also successfully completed Jungle Warfare School.

It feels pretty good to shatter a glass ceiling.

My Guiding Principles

During my challenges at West Point I began to identify my core values as a person and a leader. What is important to me as a human being? How about as a daughter, a friend, a mother? What is important to me as an employee, a manager, a mentor? Cementing your core values helps you to know what kind of a leader you are.

The core values I identified when I was young provided the basis for the guiding principles that now compose what I call my "Personal Leadership Philosophy," or PLP. My PLP is composed of five principles—core beliefs that hold me up and keep me strong whenever I am facing adversity. The idea is simple, but honing and perfecting my PLP took me over thirty years.

Principles of My Personal Leadership Philosophy

1. The Warrior Ethos: I live it every day.

> *Sometimes doing your best is not good enough.*
> *Sometimes you have to do what is required.*
> —Winston Churchill

The Warrior Ethos, as defined by the U.S. Army and taught to each Army recruit during basic training, is the standard by which American soldiers are taught to live, and the standard by which I continue to live my life today. It requires that:

- I will always place the mission first.
- I will never accept defeat.

- I will never quit.
- I will never leave a fallen comrade.

It's no coincidence that my first pillar is the Warrior Ethos. Placing the mission first, never accepting defeat, never quitting, and never leaving a fallen comrade have been important to my life both in and outside of my military service. This is the foundation of leading yourself first.

I will always place the mission first.

At Fort Hood, Texas, one of my first assignments as a platoon leader of thirty-five military policemen and women was to lead a night river-crossing exercise with a mechanized armored-division unit. It was going to be a dangerous exercise. After reporting in to the command post to get coordinating instructions and radio frequencies, I received a radio call from my company commander at headquarters to report back to the rear headquarters, about fifteen miles away through the desert terrain.

I returned to the headquarters and reported in. "Yes, sir," I said. "Is there a problem?"

He said, "Well, yes, actually, there might be a problem. When the battalion got the river-crossing mission, they asked for our best platoon leader. The only problem is, they weren't expecting a woman."

My mind began to race. *What does this comment mean, and why is he telling me now?* I thought. I replied in a puzzled manner, "Yes, sir. Are you going to relieve me of duty then?"

He paused. I think at that moment he was contemplating doing just that, but he said, "No. You know what? I'm not going to relieve you. You are going to get back out there, and you are going to kick some butt."

And I headed back out.

The whole drive back through the desert I thought about how I was under a microscope. The truth was, anyone who didn't really want me there could easily set me up for failure. When I got back to the exercise site, I talked to my platoon and told them what had happened. "We're going to do a bang-up job tonight," I encouraged them. "We're going to get everyone back home safely and have a successful mission."

The exercise went off without a hitch, and we even received a letter from the commander of that unit commending the platoon. Looking back, I am grateful that the company commander who called me back in had the courage and moral compass not to pull me from the leadership role.

I will never accept defeat.

When I was a junior officer, about twenty-nine years old, someone filed a complaint when I was hired for my first job in the National Guard. The complaint stated that a hiring official had selected me for the job over the other candidate because I was a woman. With eight years of active-duty experience and my West Point education, I was far better qualified to do the job, but I wasn't an insider, someone who had been in the Guard from day one. Plus, I was a woman, and there were very few female officers in the ranks.

The complaint made me very upset, and I couldn't help but take it personally. I spoke to a colonel in the organization, a senior leader not in my chain of command, and told him that I felt my name had been ruined and that people were already talking about me behind my back. He explained to me that in the spectrum of things, this complaint issue was really minute, and I shouldn't allow it to consume me and change my motivation to serve. He predicted that in a year, no one would even remember the complaint.

Well, he was right! His advice was a wake-up call for me. It's painful when someone criticizes you, but you have to make a choice. I chose to stay and not accept defeat.

I will never quit.

On my first day with the Georgia National Guard, as I walked by various buildings to receive my orders, I noticed a colonel standing outside enjoying the Saturday morning. He had a big, unlit stogie hanging out of his mouth and his foot propped up on a log. As I passed, he stopped me and said, "Captain Britt, come on over here."

We exchanged salutes with morning pleasantries, and he told me he was very glad that I was in the Georgia National Guard. I of course responded, "Thank you, sir. I am so proud to be here serving my country and my state."

"Yes, I'm glad you're here," he said, "because we need more good-looking women in this organization."

I was completely taken aback. I didn't know how to respond. My very first day in a new organization, and this seemingly harmless example of misogyny was how it started. I smartly saluted and offered some comment on having a nice day. I really can't remember what I said due to my shock.

Later, after I processed the situation and realized this was a forecast of what my future may look like with this organization, I called my husband and told him this wasn't going to work, that I couldn't be in an unprofessional environment like this. My husband reassured me that all of the leadership wasn't like this one example, and that the colonel was a few years from retirement. As inappropriate and unprofessional as the comment was, I realized that he may have intended it as a compliment— he did call me "good looking," after all—and that I would have to deal with "dinosaurs" like him from time to time.

I decided not to quit, and knew that I would have to exercise patience while I waited for the dinosaurs to become "extinct" by retiring one at a time. I came to appreciate the meaning of this truism: "You have to stay in the fight if you want to influence the outcome."

I will never leave a fallen comrade.

One morning, several fellow platoon leaders and I were performing the Army Physical Fitness Test (APFT) with our troops. At Fort Hood, this meant running long roads closed off to traffic on base. Our whole battalion, including company commanders and platoon leaders, was out running. A first lieutenant named Cathy was assigned as my orientation mentor, as she had a little more military leadership experience than I did and was familiar with Fort Hood. She was a decent runner, and we finished our run before many of the other soldiers in the unit. She suggested we head out a little early to get showered and back to base for our morning staff meeting. I hesitated, since so many in our company were still not done with the run, but I let her convince me it was fine to leave before all of our soldiers had crossed the finish line.

When we came back, our company commander called us both in and read us the riot act. "Where did you go?" he shouted. "You don't leave. You still had soldiers on the battlefield. They were still working. As leaders, you're the first ones there. You're the last ones to leave. Don't ever do that again."

I felt terrible because I had known better, but I let Cathy talk me into it. From that point forward, I never let someone influence me to go against my gut instinct. I trust myself and do the harder right over the easier wrong, always.

I view the term "comrade" as pertaining to those around me, whether they are family, colleagues at work, community members, or just people that float through my life at any given time. Be the type of leader who "leads from the front" with their comrades. Take the initiative. Call a friend who is down because of a divorce or death in the family. Send a card to a colleague who's recovering from surgery to let them know you care. Thank the custodians who work hard to keep your workplace sparkling. Never leaving a fallen comrade behind means lifting up those around you and letting them know you are there for them in action and in thought.

2.   Respect Others: I follow the Golden Rule.

> *I speak to everyone in the same way, whether he is*
> *the garbage man or the president of the university.*
> —Albert Einstein

Many of us learned about the Golden Rule as children: "Do unto others as you would have them do unto you." This principle has stuck with me through life, and today it is one of the five principles of my personal philosophy.

In any organization, everyone plays a key role, whether they are an individual contributor or a C-level executive. Treating others how you wish to be treated works wonders in a work environment. Can you imagine how much better professional teams could work together if everyone treated everyone else with courtesy and respect? When we treat each other with kindness, we learn to appreciate and trust each other. Team members who trust each other accomplish more together than teams where personal agendas and distrust are prevalent.

What does this mean to me as a leader? One of the most important ways I strive to embody the Golden Rule with my team is to praise publicly and punish privately. When it comes to reprimanding, I may be disappointed in someone's behavior, but I always respect the person!

Think about it. Have you ever made a mistake at your job? Did your boss or a coworker pull you aside to talk about it privately, or did he or she point it out in front of everyone at the next team meeting? The latter feels pretty uncomfortable. The former creates conversation, and that's a better place from which to move forward. When you berate somebody in public, you not only undermine any potential for a culture of openness, you also diminish yourself.

Once, when I was commanding the Georgia Army Guard, I had a senior leader who was very vocal on an issue I thought we'd already conceptually agreed upon. He was arguing a minor point in a meeting with other senior commanders in the room. I was reluctant to shut him down and make a decision without his buy-in, but I could tell the rest of the group was in agreement and ready for the decision. I looked at Bill and motioned to the door.

"Bill, let's go outside for a minute."

We went down the hallway and out of hearing range.

"Why are you arguing with me over this?" I said. "We've already talked about it. You were in total agreement last week. What happened?"

Bill, an attorney, said, "Well, I just think it'll have certain implications, and I like to argue." I appreciated his concerns and the fact that he was presenting an alternate viewpoint.

In the end, he agreed to support the action and provide me with feedback as the decision was implemented. We went back in the conference room and I said, "All right, we've discussed it and I think we're in agreement now. I understand where Bill is coming from, and I believe we were in agreement, but we had different ways of looking at it."

With that decision made, as a team we were able to move forward with the rest of our meeting and keep our focus on our mission. Because I treated Bill as I would like to be treated, we came to an agreement and maintained a professional respect for each other. Bill appreciated that when I had to see why he was disagreeing with the rest of the group, I did that with him privately.

As a parent, this guideline is important also. If your child is misbehaving, you want to hold them accountable and teach them right from wrong. You still love your child and don't want to tear down their self-confidence, but they need to know they did something wrong. You might say something like, "I love you, and you're a good daughter, but I'm very disappointed in how you acted today. You made a mistake; let's see how we can learn from that."

Whether a child or an employee, you can express disappointment and teach corrective action without disrespecting the person. Just imagine how you would feel if your roles were reversed.

3.   Give Back: It is greater to *give* than to *receive*.

> *What is the use of living, if it be not to strive for noble*
> *causes and to make this muddled world a better place*
> *for those who will live in it after we are gone?*
> —Winston Churchill

I strive to practice servant leadership—existing to serve others and work toward the greater good, not toward personal gain. Leadership is not about your own personal agenda; it's about serving for the good of the organization and continuing to develop the team.

Even in my childhood and before I knew it consciously, I was working toward a career in servant leadership. The more research I did, the more appealing the idea became—it was not just something that I knew would be a personal challenge, but something also good for women and our country. I wondered, *Can I be a woman who helps break the glass ceiling for others?*

You may not choose a career that includes being a public servant, but there are many other ways that you can give back every day. Volunteering at a local food bank, helping to care for a friend with cancer, or mentoring youth in your community are all ways to help someone else while enriching your own life with varied experiences.

You may not even realize the effect that giving back can have on you personally. One study found that people who volunteer have lower mortality rates and lower rates of depression later on in life than those who don't.[5] Find a cause you are passionate about and then get involved. There will be many reasons not to get involved, and only one reason why you should: it's the right thing to do!

4. Find Peace: I strive to live an integrated life by developing my *mind*, *body*, and *soul*.

> *Nurturing yourself is not selfish—it's essential to*
> *your survival and your well-being.*
> —Renée Peterson Trudeau

I can't be my best self unless I maintain a good mindset with a peaceful soul and a fit body. Exercise and diet are important to my mental and physical health. I work hardest to feed my soul with faith, prayer, and love of family and friends. I used to say I strove to live a balanced life, but I have realized over the years that balance is very difficult. So now I work on integration. You're going to have to go with the flow, because not everything will be in balance all the time in your life. If your soul is waning, then you need to work on the soul aspect. Sometimes you have family emergencies you need to handle. Other times you've got a job at work that demands eighteen-hour days. A personal life where the mind, body, and soul are in sync will lead to a more focused professional life.

My last job was very demanding, requiring me to work after hours and on weekends. But regardless of my workload, I'm committed to getting up every day at 5:45 a.m. to run a couple miles and do push-ups and sit-ups. No matter how late I've been up at a work event or helping my youngest daughter with schoolwork, I get up when the alarm goes off and head out the door to start my day out right, even when my mind tells me to "lie down until the motivation goes away." I know I'll feel better if I allow that exercise to fuel my body and soul. I use my exercise time to run through my mental checklist for the day and reflect on the long-term picture. I set my priorities and decide what the most important things are that I must accomplish.

For you, this means setting aside some time for yourself. That's not easy when you're busy. Try to create a routine so it will become a habit. Where can you find the time to build into your calendar an activity that brings you peace and comfort? Something as simple as being thankful each morning when your feet hit the floor can set a positive tone for your day. Perhaps setting aside time to take a walk or to spend time outside enjoying nature will fulfill you.

A study by the University of Rochester found that individuals who spent time outdoors—even just twenty minutes a day—experienced higher energy levels and feelings of happiness.[6] Look at it this way: you don't have time to be sick, so invest in staying healthy both physically and emotionally. The return on investment is amazing!

5.   Laugh Often: I look for humor in life, especially when I look at myself.

> *In three words I can sum up everything*
> *I've learned about life: it goes on.*
> —Robert Frost

Life does go on, whether we plan for it or not. As a person who prefers to be in control, it took me too many years to realize that I was missing out on the funny side of life. I didn't take time to find humor in little things or appreciate the small miracles around me. I've since learned that "perfection is the enemy of done"! Life is difficult. Take the time now to smile and look for the humor in situations you'd normally dismiss.

I once had a superior officer who in meetings always high-fived the guys when they did a great job on a project. The high five was always accompanied by a hearty "You the man!" which had been appropriate because in the past there were only men on his team. After the first few times I saw him do it, I began to wonder what he would say when I had good news to report to the team. It was only a matter of time, and my turn finally came when I announced that I had gotten a mission for overseas-deployment training with funding. He raised his hand to give me his typical gesture. "You the . . ."—he caught himself midsentence—"wo-man!"

We all smiled and laughed at the moment. He had now realized that he would have to be more aware of the slang and salutations he was using with his team, now that it was no longer made up of only men. I was proud to be the wo-man. Years later, I still chuckle when I'm in tough situations and remember, "I'm the wo-man!"

The next time you're having a challenging day, pause and reflect. Is there something funny, or at least ironic, about the situation? Is it something that you'll think is important in ten years? If not, don't sweat it. Need an excuse to laugh about something? Science has proven that laughing is good for your health![7] It can reduce stress and even help protect against heart disease.

I examine my life against the principles of my Personal Leadership Philosophy every day as I strive to live and lead to the best of my ability. My PLP works for me because I know what motivates me to find purpose in every day. I recognize that I can stay pointed toward my True North if I dig deep, am mission-minded, respect others, give back, find peace, and laugh often.

Compass Check: What Is Your Personal Leadership Philosophy?

You may not have jumped from a helicopter before or faced gender bias verging on harassment in your current workplace, but you've likely faced some professional and personal hurdles in your life. If you haven't yet, then you will. Whether you're in the boardroom, the classroom, or a military training exercise, there will come a moment when your heart is pounding because you're about to do something scary that will take you out of your comfort zone. Some may shy away from these challenges, but it's when you take the leap in the face of adversity that you learn what you're made of and become stronger. Knowing your true self and your core values will help you overcome adversity, bounce back from setbacks, and ultimately help you to lead others more effectively.

I encourage you to take a moment to identify the core values you want to uphold to maintain the course to your True North. Depending on your values, the principles of your PLP may overlap with mine, or you may have different strategies altogether for reaching your goals. Either way, you can use my principles as a model for creating your own.

Perhaps try writing down some key leadership experiences of your own, or leadership qualities that your mentors have exemplified. Don't be discouraged if you can't immediately rattle off your pillars or if you're struggling to narrow them down. What you write today doesn't have to be set in stone. It took me thirty years of trial and error before I culled down my beliefs into five.

A word of caution: writing down your philosophy won't magically transform your life. You have to be disciplined enough to follow your philosophy and turn the words on your page into action. Oftentimes we get lazy, or feel too tired or stressed to practice our philosophy to the fullest extent. Don't cheat yourself, not even by one calorie or one sit-up. Staying true to your core values, your team, and your organization is a recipe for great leaders who set themselves apart from everyone else.

The aim of the great leader is not to get people to think more highly of the leader. It's to get people to think more highly of themselves.
—Bob Moawad

III

STEP UP TO LEAD

Starter Strategies

What does it really mean to be a leader? What is it that a leader is supposed to do every day? You don't have to be leading a military force of thousands or sit at the head of a boardroom. Regardless of your position, if you are going to be a leader, there are certain basic responsibilities you will undertake.

Most assume that being a leader means holding a position where you are constantly telling your staff or team what to do all day, and then reprimanding them if they don't "get things done." If that is your definition of a leader (or a parent), then you are in for a big surprise. Leadership is much more than that. Most of it involves collaborating *with* your team, not letting them do all the work while you look down from above.

Some roles as a leader may differ, so I have established a set of precepts for which I hold myself accountable. These shape how I lead in relation to my team.

Share Your Voice, Share the Vision

When you hear the name Martin Luther King Jr., what comes to mind? For many it is his inspiring "I Have a Dream" speech. King had the vision that his children would someday live in a nation where they were not judged by the color of their skin, but by the content of their character. When Dr. King gave that speech, do you think he hoped it would live on forever as a sound bite? No. His purpose in giving that speech was to share his vision and to inspire people to come together to achieve equality. When people are inspired emotionally, they will want to come together for a purpose.

When you communicate to others as a leader, it's important that they understand your viewpoint. I keep this in mind when I know the receiver isn't going to want to hear what I have to say. But if I establish a shared value, like Dr. King, I can find my voice with confidence.

Before the other responsibilities of being a leader can fall into place, you must give your team a reason to want to be led by you. In their book *The Leadership Challenge*, James M. Kouzes and Barry Z. Posner write, "If you don't believe in the messenger, you won't believe the message." Is your message strong and worthy of others' support? Are you sharing with them the mission and goals of the company or organization? Are you helping them to understand why you are taking the team in a certain direction? Like Dr. King, are you speaking from the heart? Effectively conveying the mission and why the mission is important to the organization can help inspire your staff or team to want to work alongside you to achieve success. By adhering to the vision and shared values, and your own Personal Leadership Philosophy, you can start moving the organization in the direction it needs to go.

I was honored to serve as the founding president of the inaugural Georgia Chapter of Women in Defense. Established in July of 2015, the chapter has a mission to cultivate and support the advancement and recognition of women in all aspects of national security. We accomplish this mission by providing a formal environment for professional growth through education, networking, and career development. Many presumed the group was for military women. Although men and women in uniform are encouraged to join, it's much larger than our military segment. The chapter exists to support all facets of defense, including the technology industrial base, defense businesses, or those who want to do business with the government, academia, and government agencies. The board and I felt it was important to add a clarifying sentence to the mission statement to help potential members understand their value to the organization. The additional sentence states: "Members of this nonprofit National Security Organization, inclusive of men and women, share interests in fields related to security and defense of the state of Georgia and the United States."

Sometimes the mission can seem unclear to new members or to the public, so by adding a clarifying statement you can help connect the dots for your organization and those who are interested in being aligned with you. As the leader, I had to make the mission relevant to our members and explain both the greater good to our state and nation and to them individually. I enjoyed watching people's faces light up once they understood the chapter's mission and how they fit into the big picture. This excitement translates into wanting to be a part of the organization and a willingness to volunteer time and resources to contribute to a worthy cause.

Set Priorities to Focus Your Resources

The leader is responsible for guiding the team in the direction of achieving the mission. Every task or mission, whether personal or professional, is going to have a set of priorities, and at times it can be overwhelming for members of your team to know what ranks as most important. During my time with the Georgia Army National Guard, some of the priorities that I established for the team were improving our deployment readiness, enhancing our facilities, bettering our logistical planning process, and more. Once I had determined the priorities, it was my responsibility to share the message of these goals with the team and also to be sure that we were maximizing the resources being used to accomplish these goals.

There are going to be times when it will feel like everything is a priority, but as a leader you will have to narrow it down to only a few that are critical to the core mission of the organization. It's up to the leader to be sure to direct their team in understanding priorities. A lot of time can be wasted by a leader who doesn't know where they want to "go."

Remember the Cheshire Cat in *Alice in Wonderland*? When Alice comes to a fork in the road and asks the cat which way to go, he tells her it depends on where she's trying to get to. "I don't much care where," Alice tells him. And then the cat says to her, "Then it doesn't matter which way you go."[8]

You should always have a vision for the direction of your team, company, and family, and you should take them along the road that reaches or accomplishes that vision. While you and your team will each have your *own* True North, your company, organization, or team may also have a True North that you are working toward achieving, such as increasing membership, growing revenue, improving diversity, etc.

Reading the Wind: Plan for the Worst, Hope for the Best

Colin Powell once said that when selecting someone to join your organization, "Look for intelligence and judgment and, most critically, a capacity to anticipate, to see around corners."[9] Being able to "see around corners" means you are able to anticipate what might be possible even though you can't actually see the full path ahead. I practice this skill while sailing, something I've been passionate about since my West Point days. When navigating my sailboat, I have to watch and predict the impact of winds and adjust my next move to maximize speed and trajectory of motion. In essence, it's like seeing around corners to be ready for the next move. In my past positions, that is exactly what I have done—anticipate the problems that might come down the road, whether it was with the Georgia Army National Guard or the university. As a leader, your job is to hone your ability to see what may lie ahead. Not only can this practice help avoid potential pitfalls or failures in the future, it can also strengthen the core of the organization along the way.

During my service with the Georgia Army National Guard, I spent years advocating for preventative-healthcare measures for soldiers.

Shortly after 9/11, I was selected to be the G1 director of personnel for the Georgia Army National Guard. I was responsible for the recruitment and retention of soldiers, maintaining a certain level of strength in numbers, increasing personal readiness for individual skill training, and medical and dental readiness. With Operation Iraqi Freedom looming, the main focus was on getting soldiers trained in marksmanship and special skills, such as vehicle maintenance or medical response, but little focus was placed on ensuring the physical health and wellness of the soldiers before they headed off into the field. All the training in the world wouldn't help if a soldier was deemed unable to deploy to the battlefield due to a health issue. Addressing personnel medical and dental health had to become a priority, and early on. A soldier can't focus properly on their mission if they are not healthy. Prior to this time, medical and dental readiness was assessed and taken care of just before deployment. Once deployment is planned, there's not much time to heal the soldiers as they prepare to leave their jobs and loved ones behind.

Many Guard soldiers don't have dental insurance. If a soldier had not been receiving good dental care prior to a scheduled deployment, sometimes the only option left for a dentist getting them ready to ship out overseas within the next few days was to pull a tooth. Once overseas they would not have regular medical and dental care, and a bad tooth couldn't be left to create more problems for the soldier. After watching our men and women get on airplanes with gauze in their mouths from just having teeth pulled out, I knew we could be doing better.

Over the next ten years, I made it my mission to improve the care of our Guard soldiers. For dental care we set up Operation Healthy Smiles, changing the drill halls into dentist offices. We brought dentists in and they would set up their whole office, doing extractions, fillings, crowns, exams, cleanings . . . whatever was needed. We set up an intense rotation for soldiers. Now if they were going to deploy, we were able to take care of their needs early enough that drastic measures weren't needed just before shipping out.

The month that I left service, September of 2011, the Georgia National Guard hit number one for medical and dental readiness in the United

States. As someone who practices servant leadership, I knew that we had needed to do a better job of serving the men and women who were volunteering to risk their lives for us in times of need. As a leader, that's what you do. You fight for the resources and for your troops. Largely because of this effort, I later received the Distinguished Service Medal.

At the university, one of my passions was public health and emergency preparedness. When the news of the Zika scare began to break, I knew that we needed to get the campus prepared for any possible issue that could arise. Many details about the virus were still in the early stages of discovery, but I knew that it was critical to start preparing as soon as possible, especially since Zika has no preventative vaccine or known cure. With diseases, you never know how fast something can spread or an outbreak can form in a new area.

I had already established a public-health advisory committee on campus, so I convened the committee to help create our Zika plans. We were one of the first universities in Georgia to put together formal plans for how to prevent and then handle a possible outbreak of the virus. We began sharing information on the virus and the latest updates from the Centers for Disease Control on the university's website. We met with the state's entomologist to discuss mosquito prevention, mapped out a plan of spraying the campus to reduce mosquitoes, and addressed areas that had chronic water stagnation. Special health-risk briefings were set up for study-abroad students. We arranged for a supply of insect-repellant pens for interested students and launched an educational campaign. We also put a pandemic plan into place—what we would do if a major outbreak occurred. I tried to "see around corners" and plan for the worst case if and when Zika hit the state of Georgia.

Regardless of your field or position, there may be aspects of your role that could benefit from an ability to "see around corners." What can you predict and plan for that others won't even think to prepare for? How many steps ahead are you of others in your organization in terms of readiness for errors that may occur, a shift in financial status, or a new trend in your industry? The skill of seeing around corners is something that you'll likely hone over time as you train yourself to think beyond the current circumstances to what lies ahead.

Be with People Who Want to Excel and Achieve

The best teams are made up of members who are mission-minded and dig their heels in to accomplish the shared vision. When everyone on a team is the kind of person who wants to excel and achieve in life, you're going to be able to make progress and see projects through to completion. As a leader who understands the "bigger picture," I look for people who can see things from a strategic and operational perspective, so our team can focus on the future of our organization together. Those who are good with strategic and operational thinking can best support my efforts to manage the overall arc of a project.

I'm sure you can think back to an organization or team that you've been a part of that was full of go-getters. Perhaps you've also been part of one that easily lost focus or felt stagnant. As a leader, don't be afraid to change up the members. I strive to surround myself with people who want to excel and achieve, because those are the people who get the job done.

Besides wanting to surround yourself with high achievers, you should strive to be someone that others want to have around them. Remember being a kid in gym class when it was time to pick teams? Were you one of the first picked, or one of the last? Those who are never asked to contribute or get passed over for the next person should ask themselves why. Showing initiative is key to career advancement. Be that aggressive, action-oriented person that others want to have on their team.

Have a "Tenth Man/Woman"

General George Patton once said, "If everyone is thinking alike, someone isn't thinking!" As a leader, it is up to you to put together a staff or team of people who don't all think alike. It may feel tempting and comfortable to surround yourself with "yes-men (or women)" who will all go with the flow. If everyone agrees, then work is easier and things get done more effectively . . . right? Wrong. You need a devil's advocate (or two) in your group—someone who is brave enough to speak up with a different opinion.

The "tenth man" rule is a concept practiced by some in business, where if nine people completely agree on a strategy or plan, then a tenth person is needed who will disagree or have an opposing view, to help find flaws or holes in the strategy. You must have people who think differently around you. I refer to this as "diversity of thought." It can be a challenge as a leader to seek a variety of thinkers who may not see eye to eye with you or with anyone else on the team, but ultimately the solution will be better thought out and have more buy-in from the people impacted by the decision.

This approach brings to mind the movie *World War Z*, in which an Israeli general warns that the country should prepare for a zombie invasion. The others may have thought it seemed crazy to prepare for zombies—something that had never been encountered before—but by throwing out an idea that went against the grain, the general helped save lives. He gave the other "team members" something else to consider, something to prepare for that they had not thought about.

Keep in mind you don't literally need a tenth person to make this work. It's all about the leader of a group encouraging diversity of thought. Recruit people from a variety of backgrounds. Be sure that the team respects each person for their differences, and that each member of the team feels comfortable in sharing an opinion that maybe goes against the grain.

Running Effective Committees

Most leaders are also going to be responsible at one time or another for forming and leading committees or teams for special projects. Committees are often formed to solve multidisciplinary problems, or problems that may impact a number of departments or sectors within an organization. Very often these teams or committees will have people on them whom you have never worked with before. It's important to have a clear and focused process when assembling your committee or team. Since this committee is likely not part of every member's day-to-day responsibilities, it's critical to maximize the time you have together. I have an agenda format that has worked well for me over the years. You can find it in the Appendix.

The first step to running an effective committee is to define the purpose of the committee. What is the problem you are setting out to resolve? Your purpose should be as specific and narrowly focused as possible. For example, the purpose could be to revise or create a new policy for reporting safety incidents. Or perhaps it is to launch a new employee incentive program.

Next, what are the deliverables? Describe what you plan to accomplish with the committee. Examples could include a draft policy, a list of candidates for a new job, a planned response to an inquiry, establishing goals for a new year, making cuts to a planned budget, or consensus on a concept that is contentious.

As the committee leader, you will have to keep the committee members on task. Adhere to the agenda you have prepared, but be ready to capture worthwhile ideas that surface in the discussion. Establish ground rules for all meetings that will be held. Here are the ground rules that have worked well for me:

1. *Agree to disagree . . . and mean it!* The team needs to know that they will not be criticized for their counterarguments, and likewise, they shouldn't judge others. Everyone on the committee should accept that they will not agree on everything discussed or decided. Constructive disagreement is healthy to reaching a well-thought-out solution.

2. *Listen first to understand, then speak.* Truly listen and make sure you understand what someone else is saying before you counter or respond. Committee members can become so focused on what they want to say that they don't hear the other person's position. Team members need to be sure they truly understand what other members are saying before they have an immediate reaction.

3. *Let the speaker finish his or her thought.* Everyone should have a chance to speak without being interrupted so that they can calmly and clearly convey their idea or suggestion. This creates a safe zone for those who may be reluctant to share for fear of being rudely interrupted. It is critical for those in a meeting to feel like they are in a "safe zone," especially for people who may be too

shy or too polite to speak up and share their opinions or ideas with others.

4. *Keep the discussion on topic during the meeting.* Time is valuable and certain tasks have to be accomplished before a meeting ends, so to stay productive don't let the group get off track. My tip? Offer to set up a "Parking Lot" for ideas that surface but are not adding value to the issue at hand. I normally have a butcher paper pad or an electronic note taker to capture ideas and move on. If someone goes on a tangent, remind them of the limited meeting time but value their idea by adding it to the "Parking Lot" to be addressed sometime in the future.

5. *Park your ego and agendas at the door.* No single member's thoughts, ideas, or suggestions are more important than anyone else's on the committee. Each member's contribution should have equal consideration by the committee. The group will seldom achieve its assigned mission if there are members who are set on pushing their own agendas.

6. *Call for alibi fire.* As a leader and mentor, my role is to encourage risk-taking and learning, and to continuously teach. I welcome and value input from all colleagues and employees. They should share ideas and not feel persecuted for throwing an idea out there that some may see as "crazy." We have a term in the military called "alibi fire," which is where you empty the clip of your gun downrange if you have bullets remaining in your weapon after a timed firing exercise. At the end of a meeting, I call for "alibi fire" and go around the table, having everyone give me their thoughts and feedback. It's their final chance in the meeting to express any opinions, ideas, or countering points they have on a topic or issue. It also encourages team members to stay engaged throughout the meeting. I have found when I call "alibi fire" that it's usually the point at which women speak up. Being called upon to speak in each meeting helps give them the encouragement they need to contribute while knowing that they are in a safe environment free of judgment.

Have an Open Door

Leaders are often balancing many tasks at one time, making it difficult to keep an ear to the ground when it comes to certain issues. How many times have you heard about an employee or customer issue indirectly from another department? To combat this, I have an open-door policy in which anyone in the organization can get messages to me unfiltered. If your team and employees feel comfortable talking to you about anything, they are less likely to file a formal complaint or go to the media about an issue, giving you a chance to help reach a resolution faster, and saving a lot of potential headaches.

Jumping the chain of command is often frowned upon; however, listening and acknowledging concerns will often solve the issue and keep it from escalating unnecessarily. When I was commanding the Georgia Army National Guard, there were many leaders who did not like that I had an open-door policy. The mentees who were coming to me were going two to three levels up in the chain of command by coming to me when they could have been going to others. It made certain leaders feel threatened, causing me to wonder, *What are they hiding? What are they afraid will happen? Are they listening and understanding the pulse of their unit or department?* Letting colleagues and subordinates know they are welcome to come and speak to me freely promotes trust and transparency in the organization. I always feel that it is better to know the information firsthand and early on, especially if it's "bad."

Be careful not to overreact to information. It took me years to realize that there are always two sides to every story and that first reports, especially in the media, are often inaccurate. Be patient and consider the consequences of your actions, especially if you need to protect the confidentiality of an employee.

Create a Safe Culture of Reporting

Your team needs to feel comfortable bringing issues to you, so as a leader you will need to create a culture of safe reporting. This practice applies regardless of the type of issue, be it project-based, financial, interpersonal, etc. As a leader, you will need to be aware of everything happening in your organization, both good and bad.

The CEO of school bus manufacturer Blue Bird, Phil Horlock, once said, "If you beat the heck out of people when there's bad news, guess what—they don't want to tell you what's going on any more. That's why companies go into tailspins, because the issues don't surface. You have to create an environment where people put the issues on the table."[10] Horlock's former boss at Ford, Alan Mulally, had taught him that "you can't manage a secret." In layman's terms: if you don't know about something, you won't be able to take steps to deal with it.

If your environment is such that your team is not comfortable reporting issues to you, problems can spiral out of control before you are able to deal with them effectively. If they know that their concerns will be heard, the members of your team who care about the organization will speak up, putting you in a position to make things right. If they feel that things won't change even if an issue is brought up, they'll function under an "if it ain't broke, don't fix it" attitude, and that is not something you want your team to have if you're trying to grow your organization or move it forward.

When an issue is reported, be sure that you are treating any parties involved fairly and that you are hearing all sides of the story before taking action. You want to make sure that all members of the organization continue to feel comfortable reporting issues or concerns to leadership. Don't "shoot the messenger" who brings the problem to your attention. Focus the discussion and response on the issue or problem, not necessarily who brought it to your attention or whose "fault" it is. "Fix the problem, not the blame."[11]

As the Georgia Army National Guard commander, I required quarterly readiness briefings with trend indicators. After a few briefings, I questioned why certain units were showing as "red," or poorly prepared in terms of their readiness for deployment, and had not shown any improvement with the additional resourcing being placed for dental and medical readiness. After pushing for an answer, I was told that those units had a higher ratio of female soldiers. I asked for more explanation. I was told that "women are more complicated and have special exams." It is true that there are different medical readiness standards and tests for female soldiers than male soldiers, such as mammograms and pelvic exams, but that was no reason for the commanders, myself included, to not figure out how to get all of our soldiers ready to deploy.

Now that I knew what the "secret" was, I could better align resources to address the issue. Mammogram and female-healthcare vans with doctors were brought to armories around the state on drill weekends to give scans and medical exams to the deploying soldiers at no cost. The headquarters' medical team collaborated with OB/GYN doctors in specific areas to offer vouchers for payment of medical services if female soldiers were unable to use the vans due to training requirements.

Within the next two quarters, the "red" units were now "yellow" or "green" and trending up. The female soldiers received the screening tests or the care they needed, and were then able to step up as contributing members of their unit. The predominantly male leadership was ill at ease with discussing female issues, in part because I was a woman. I listened and appreciated their unease. Afterward, I created separate metrics for tracking female-soldier readiness, creating a safe culture for commanders to discuss tough or uncomfortable issues.

Challenge Employees (They Expect It!)

If you haven't noticed, I have very high expectations for my teams. But I also tend to have high-achieving teams, and I don't think that's a coincidence! A leader's job is to push his or her employees by expecting more out of them, giving them challenging tasks, and driving them to find the strength and courage they didn't know they had in themselves. As employees are empowered to stretch their skill set, monitor their progress and coach them along the way. Be a sounding board for their ideas. Encourage them to rehearse a presentation with you as the audience.

Your feedback should have both positive points and areas they can improve upon. Be honest with compassion, sharing your goal of wanting to make them better prepared to serve the organization. Some may recoil at the initial feedback, but I have found that over the long term, they mature as leaders and embrace the counsel, appreciating the honesty and the leader who gave it.

Teach to Achieve the Standard

Like many of my bosses have done for me, you must take an interest in others' professional development. Be willing to take on mentees and share lessons you've learned to help them be successful. I have had many people whom I mentored years ago reconnect with me and tell me that the extra time I took out of my busy schedule to help them develop made a big difference in their career trajectory.

When your employees ask you for help, help them, even if it means finding them a position with another team in your organization. (Sometimes that's the best way for an employee to grow.) Often your team will be composed of members who need to hone their skill sets to do their best work for you. When that's the case, take the initiative to become their teacher. Focus on those who display the most potential, regardless of gender, race, background, etc. One might think that as a woman I would have mentored far more women than men, but looking back I recall having mentored just as many men as women.

Develop a performance improvement plan together. Provide additional training or guidance to help them grow in their role. Suggest additional resources they can utilize. If you can't teach them certain skills, help them get the extra training they need. Find out what classes are available through human resources, or send them to a seminar or webinar. Assign a mentor to them, or suggest they meet with a colleague to share best practices. Set up a shadowing opportunity within the organization so that they can learn what upper-level positions entail or what skills they should be acquiring to better themselves to reach a certain level. If they seem reluctant to grow in their position, make a case for why their development is vital to their future. Stagnation is not a good option for the individual or the organization. I have learned that if you're not moving forward, then you're falling behind. This is true of honing your skill set, earning education degrees, and keeping up with technology.

Build Self-Image/Confidence

Legend has it that a passerby once asked Michelangelo what made him want to carve a rock into an angel. Michelangelo replied, "I saw the angel in the marble and carved until I set him free." As a leader, I strive to carve out the goodness and strengths in every employee. And while I'm doing that, I try to help them counter the negatives—in other words, strengthen their weaknesses. I do this by helping them understand where their weaknesses are and how they are perceived by others. I work to maximize the impact of goodness in people while minimizing the impact of their weaknesses.

Before carving out the goodness, you will want to observe the person and understand their capabilities and motivations. Once you're confident you have a solid assessment, involve the person in a leadership role outside of their normal routine. Examples can include asking them to assist you with a project outside of their department or offering them a new leadership role of a committee. The change allows them to practice their leadership style, gain experience, and grow in confidence. Encourage risk-taking and expect mistakes to be made. Encourage employees to learn from their mistakes and discover preventive measures to avoid the same pitfalls again. I have said to my teams, "I don't mind if you make mistakes, just don't make them twice!"

You want confident people who feel good about contributing and doing that extra research. Developing an atmosphere where the team is learning and growing from mistakes versus a zero-tolerance environment is how an organization becomes stronger and more successful. Leaders will often see the potential in an employee before the employee sees it in him or herself. Carve it out!

Compass Check: Your Leadership Role Evolves

You may go in to a leadership position knowing many specifics of your role, but be prepared for change. When sailing, I have to set my sails in the right direction to capture the wind and propel the boat. As with opportunities, the winds will shift and come from unexpected directions. You will have to be ready to take advantage of the new wind while staying on course to reach your destination.

Leaders have numerous roles that evolve, or ebb and flow with the needs of the organization. Here are examples of the most notable roles: visionary, decision maker, change manager, role model leading by example, confidence builder in the brand and people, cheerleader inspiring and energizing the team, communicator that's both open and honest, empathizer listening to understand, team builder, coach offering feedback, teacher helping teams make better decisions, and monitor of progress with continuous self-improvement.

Experience, faith, and confidence will drive your decisions on the role you need to prioritize and the direction you must steer the organization. Chart your course, but like the captain of a boat, be adaptable. Prepare yourself and your organization to take advantage of the unexpected winds.

If you advance within an organization, think of what you are required to do in your new role compared to your previous one. Are any responsibilities or functions the same? Are any different? As you continue to advance into new roles, understand that change is going to be a constant factor.

If there is currently a leadership role you are aspiring to achieve, take a few minutes to brainstorm or list out what responsibilities come with the role. But think outside the box. Like the examples I have given in this chapter, think about your role as a leader while keeping in mind the bigger picture in your organization or industry. Prepare yourself mentally, and then go for it!

The greater danger for most of us lies not in setting our aim too high and falling short, but in setting our aim too low, and achieving our mark.
—Michelangelo

IV

FIGURE IT OUT

Develop Your Leadership Style

G reat leaders have personal guidelines they follow when conducting themselves in a professional setting. An effective leader is almost always known by their colleagues and staff to think, act, and therefore lead in a consistent manner. They have a certain "style" of leadership. Some aspects of their style have been developed slowly over the course of their career—maybe due to trial and error—while others have come by instinct.

For me personally, the foundation of my leadership style was developed during my time at West Point, but I have also grown a great deal and adapted since then, incorporating fundamentals I have learned from professional positions and aspects of my personal life. Staying focused on my True North has helped to ensure that my leadership style drives me in the direction of achieving my personal and professional goals.

As you read through this chapter, consider how these style fundamentals could have a positive impact on your leadership style.

Set Standards and Communicate Them

As the leader, your team is looking to you for guidance. Let them know up front what your expectations are. If your team members know what is expected of them, they'll also know that you'll communicate with them if they're not meeting expectations. Set standards and educate your employees on them. Don't accept mediocrity; all that does is breed more mediocrity. If someone on your team is delivering the bare minimum, others will take that as a sign that they, too, can deliver the minimum, and then never push themselves to excel. Set the bar high for all members of your team, encouraging them to make more impactful achievements with each assignment. Team members should feel some pressure to keep up with their colleagues, maintaining an overall high level of success for the team.

One of the best ways to communicate those expectations is to be a role model yourself. By leading yourself first in your work, staying on task, meeting deadlines, and contributing thoughtful value, you project an image of how your team should perform. Sometimes I have to gently remind my team to review those expectations again. Occasionally, pulling someone aside is necessary.

I communicate my standards to new team members by meeting with them shortly after they are hired. I present new hires with copies of my Personal Leadership Philosophy (PLP) and my Leadership Credo,[i] which outlines the standards and best practices I have set for myself as a leader. I then engage them in a discussion about my leadership style and how I expect them to present themselves in their role within the organization. They leave the meeting with a clear understanding of my expectations and a better sense of how they contribute to the big picture. The discussion also gives me insight into their leadership preferences and motivations. After gaining a glimpse of how I lead, they are more likely to feel confident and ready to start fully participating as a leader in the organization.

[i] Various portions of the Leadership Credo are discussed throughout this chapter and the book. For a one-page summary of my Leadership Credo, see the Appendix.

Don't Micromanage—Provide Guidance

Once you communicate your expectations, let your team get to work. Don't micromanage them, but simply provide clear and concise guidance. Sam Walton, founder of Walmart, advised, "Communicate everything you possibly can to your partners. The more they know, the more they'll understand. The more they understand, the more they'll care. Once they care, there's no stopping them."[12] When you micromanage, you don't empower, and employees sense you don't trust them. It's much better to gain buy-in and consensus by sharing knowledge rather than hoarding it and giving directives. As a good leader, you have to trust your team to do their respective jobs to the best of their ability while monitoring the progress.

When additional guidance is required, I will question a team member with, "Do you understand what we're trying to accomplish with this project? Let's go back to the intent. Can I clarify the priorities or goals for you?" I make sure that team members have a clear understanding of the organization or team's shared vision. Once people understand what you're trying to accomplish, they'll be on board with helping you achieve the vision.

Be Patient, Especially When Listening

When you first make the transition into leadership, you will likely feel a bit tense, maybe stressed, and rushed. It can be difficult to take a step back and be patient with your team and yourself. You've been given tasks, goals, or a mission to accomplish by your upper management, and you are focused on that and nothing else. You may also feel that you can accomplish certain tasks better or faster than the team that is now working for you. This is where patience—or as I like to call it, "tactical patience"—is critical. In order to have a good working relationship with your team, you will have to be patient with them as they contemplate decisions, make mistakes, and then learn and grow. This can be one of the most difficult practices for many new leaders.

One common misperception about leaders is that they make decisions in a vacuum and then direct the implementation. However, nothing can be further from the truth. Effective leadership must be collaborative, persuasive, and lead to buy-in from those implementing the decision, i.e. your employees. As leaders work through this process, they will be challenged to exercise patience and be receptive to feedback. Listening is often underrated, but essential to making good decisions. Someone once told me that God gave us two ears and one mouth so we could listen twice the amount we talk. This saying keeps me grounded and makes me laugh at myself when I become impatient.

Listening is a skill that is lost on many people in today's professional environment. And it is indeed a skill. When you move into a leadership role, not only will your responsibilities have increased, but so will the number of people with whom you interact, be they colleagues, higher-ups, or your staff. It can be easy to fall into a trap of being "busy" and getting annoyed with additional demands on your time. But by listening to your staff and colleagues, their feedback will become a valuable part of your growth and success as a leader. Be careful not to create a perception that you are too busy to listen to your staff and colleagues, as this may lead to them withholding suggestions, feedback, or concerns—impeding good decision-making and hurting the organization.

One of the toughest challenges I faced while working in higher education was creating a policy that would reduce the safety risk in "experiential learning activities"—off-campus activities meant to enhance student learning in their chosen fields. A sense of urgency manifested in Georgia colleges and universities after a horrific traffic accident killed five Georgia Southern nursing students in 2015. The students were on the highway, traveling to a hospital for their final clinical session of the semester, when a tractor trailer slammed into their two vehicles, killing five of the seven students. The university I worked for at the time had already begun a policy prior to this accident at the urging of one of the deans, who, ironically, was concerned about nursing students traveling off campus. It turned out no other major university in the state had a policy to mitigate experiential-learning risk either.

For months, our risk-reduction committee collaborated and got close to what I thought was a commonsense policy that had a basic risk-assessment checklist for faculty and staff. However, a senior university official stepped in and said that I needed more faculty input into our policy to earn their buy-in. I solicited volunteers from among the faculty who would be impacted by the policy. Many gladly engaged, knowing they had a chance to shape a policy they would have to live with. It was a tough crowd, many with their own personal agendas, and I soon realized the majority of the faculty were against the policy. Now I understood why that senior university official had urged me to gather this group, and I was better prepared to listen to their feedback.

I pushed the group of faculty members to help me understand why giving a risk-assessment checklist and prescripted safety briefings for them to review with their students prior to off-campus activities was unpopular. One voice emerged with something I hadn't considered. He told me that by creating a policy and a checklist, I was now making them personally responsible and liable if something happened. I was so focused on a policy to impact the greater good that I didn't consider the individual fears it might create. The attorney on the team reassured them that they were not personally liable should an incident occur, and questioned what faculty member wouldn't want to create a safer learning environment for themselves and their students. In light of this information and by discussing the individual concerns, the group reached consensus that a policy would be a helpful tool moving forward.

Even when it seems nearly impossible, collaboration is critical in any organization. Be patient and understand that not everyone will immediately be on the same page. Remember that "tenth man/woman" discussed earlier? When folks are contributing opinions or ideas to the conversation that you may not want to bother listening to, try to consider where each individual is coming from and appreciate the perspective they give. When a team feels that their input was heard by leadership and has been used in the creation of a new policy or procedure, they're more likely to support the new measures than if they feel like their input wasn't valued.

Don't Offer or Accept Excuses—There Aren't Any Good Ones

While I want to understand both sides of a story, what I don't want to hear are excuses for shortfalls or mistakes. We all make mistakes; if you don't, then you're probably not trying hard enough. Despite our best intentions, sometimes things slip through the cracks. My preference is that rather than give an excuse, admit you have made a mistake and own it. My only request is that you learn from it and don't let it happen again. As a leader, I ultimately have to own the outcomes of my team. It's counterproductive to cast blame or throw any individual "under the bus." Instead, take the high road and accept responsibility as the leader. You will earn your team's respect and trust while encouraging risk-taking and high performance.

As a plebe (the West Point term for freshman), there were only three responses we could give our superiors: "Yes, sir," "No, sir," or "No excuse, sir." Even though I always wanted to tell my squad leader what happened, I learned quickly that the best response was "No excuse, sir." That was a great lesson to start off my training as a leader. I realized that excuses were a crutch to shift responsibility for one's actions. There is always a way to explain yourself without making an excuse. Oftentimes the truth is the best and easiest answer to give. If you catch yourself frequently making excuses, consider it a sign that it's time to make a change in your habits or actions to keep from making more excuses in the future.

I once had an employee who was always two minutes late to every meeting. She would come in the door with too many bags in her hands, struggle to take her coat off, and shuffle through all her papers to find something to take notes on. Although a superstar, she was never prepared enough to brief the team on her projects. She always wondered how the rest of the team found the time to prepare each week. Her excuse about "not having enough time to do her job as everyone else" only hurt her own credibility and insulted her colleagues. After noticing a pattern, I pulled her aside and let her know that with a few small actions that required minor effort, such as tracking her projects on a rolling list a few days before, she could come to the meeting equally prepared. Women tend to carry more bags or items than men, especially their purse. I'm also guilty of this, so I come prepared with a folder and laptop for reference. I arrive at the meeting place five minutes early, take my coat off ahead of time, and walk into the boardroom with a show of confidence. Own it!

A Half-Truth Is a Whole Lie—Be Straight Up with Me

Demand honesty from your employees at all times. A half-truth is a whole lie! Leaders have to ask the right questions to see through the half-truths. It's a delicate balance to trust and empower your employees while ensuring you are getting the entire picture of a situation. I delve in by asking, "Is there anything else that impacts this situation?" as an open-ended invitation to discuss points that the messenger may consider minor or less relevant. Whether or not it's intentional, not providing all the information around an issue can cause the leader to make an uninformed decision that sets the entire team up for failure.

If you do have a team member who lies intentionally, find out why immediately. Lying is an indication that the team member has motives disconnected from the organization or the mission, and that is not someone you want to keep on your team for much longer.

Go Bold or Go Home

Have you ever been in a situation where you *have* to step up as a leader . . . but you're totally uncomfortable with the moment? You're already committed to speak before a group or you're put on the spot to make comments at a meeting and your confidence is lacking. You have just seconds to rise to the occasion. Buck up and "go bold," because it's too late to "go home"!

Once, when I was a plebe at West Point, I was out for a morning jog across the parade field, an area where you're not allowed to step on the grass. Once you start on the path, you don't have any escape options to avoid someone along the way. Taking that path was a decision that meant I could encounter either someone I would have to salute, or someone who could harass me. During my jog I saw a figure coming toward me through the eerie fog. It startled me a bit, and I wanted to turn back, but the figure had seen that I was there, and I wasn't going to turn around and retreat. I knew I would need to give the greeting of the day. There are different greetings for each level of classmen or officer you encounter. I quickly ran through my head the scenarios as the figure came closer through the fog.

Suddenly, I realized that the person coming closer to me was *the* superintendent of West Point, Lieutenant General Andrew Goodpaster, a three-star general. He had been brought back to help with the transition of integrating women at the academy, so I was part of the reason he was back at the school after retiring years before. My time at West Point thus far had been trying, and many officers had treated me and my fellow female cadets poorly. Knowing a legend was approaching me on this narrow path made me both proud and nervous. I think he must have been able to see the look of total distress on my face. He looked at me, we locked eyes, and he just smiled. I will never forget that smile. I popped the appropriate salute and said, "Good morning, sir." He saluted back and kept on going.

My heart was pounding in my chest—I felt sure I was having a heart attack. Once I calmed down, I was hit with a realization. For me to be out there in that early-morning fog with a three-star general was reaffirming. It was uplifting to know that someone at that high of a level could still treat a young cadet like me as a human being. This was over thirty-five years ago, and I still remember that smile. He has since passed away, and I cried when I learned of his death. He was a great man, and his work at the academy was important to the inclusion of women in the military.

But what if I *had* turned back? What if I hadn't stood my ground, stepped out of my comfort zone, and ran off in another direction? I would not have gotten that subconscious reassurance of my time and presence at West Point, a memory that has stuck with me to this day. Recalling this moment is like my own personal pep talk that gives me the courage to mingle with an unknown crowd or give a presentation to an unreceptive audience. Once you commit to doing something, do it with confidence. If you're half-hearted, then you shouldn't do it at all. That's what the simple but impactful phrase means: "Go bold or go home!"

Be Willing to Take Risks

There is a reason there are so many motivational quotes related to the concept of taking risks, such as "Nothing ventured, nothing gained," "No risk, no reward," "No pain, no gain," and more. That's because it's a proven concept. When you move into a leadership role, you are going to be faced with very difficult decisions, and difficult decisions often require big choices. Make the right choice and it can pay off in a big way. Make the wrong choice and there may be some consequences, but even so you will have learned a very valuable lesson along the way.

You should not only be willing to take risks yourself, but work with your team on the value of risk-taking as well. Coach them on what risks are acceptable and what risks are nonnegotiable, depending on the type of organization you are with and its mission. Give your team examples from your industry—or even your own career—of some risks that paid off in a big way, and others that didn't quite work out as expected.

One of the biggest risks I have taken in my career was accepting a position in higher education as an associate vice president for operations. It was a huge shift in my career path. The years of military experience and leadership did not guarantee success in this new position. I had been replaced as the commander of the Georgia Army National Guard just a few months earlier, and my only experience in higher education was as a student. What I did have were strong leadership skills, an understanding of youth, self-confidence, and a desire to succeed. I knew that if I dedicated myself to the role and encompassed all I had learned in my career up to that point that I would serve the organization well. But as many of us often feel when doing something we have never done before, there was self-doubt and a fear of failure in the back of my mind.

Am I good enough? Can I do this?

Fortunately, my future boss was prior military and understood the value of my skill set and leadership ability. He was a strong and established leader at the university, and would teach me what I didn't know while opening opportunities for me to get the training or networking needed to compensate for experience gaps. He was able to see around corners and realize the synergy of our leadership styles and experiences. Some at the university may have thought he was taking a risk in selecting me rather than someone with years of experience in an education setting. As a selfless leader, he understood the value of my servant leadership and the fresh ideas I would bring to the university. His institutional knowledge paired with my "newness" to the industry made us a strong team. His willingness to take a risk on me motivated me to work smarter. It was a calculated risk that paid off for the department and the university.

When You Bring Up a Problem, Offer Solutions

I have found that the best solutions often come from those who are closest to the problem. That's why I am up front with employees and encourage them to bring me options and possible solutions when they bring a problem to my attention. I recognize that I'm not smart enough to solve all the problems of the organization. Oftentimes, it's more important as a leader to ask the right questions than to try to provide answers. Asking the probing questions will help the owner of the issue look beyond the solutions to the consequences.

If an employee raises a problem without offering options, I will ask, "What are some ways we could approach this?" or "Who could we benchmark?" or "What do our competitors do?" Normally I will not make a snap decision without getting a complete picture of the situation and facts. This forces your team members to do their homework first and develop their own recommendations. They also experience buy-in because they were part of the discussion and the solution, and therefore feel more invested in the success of the solution. It's a learning experience for everyone involved.

Early in my military career, I had a boss who felt only he could solve the issue. Subordinates in his department would bring him their problems or issues knowing he would willingly take them on and lighten their load. As much as the leader saw this as a sign of strong leadership, I viewed it as people taking advantage of his controlling style and reducing his effectiveness to be strategic. Be careful not to let your staff use you or your role as a "dumping ground" for issues. If this is happening to you, your time can quickly evaporate while solving issues other competent leaders should be empowered to solve. In giving me the issues to deal with, I realized that my staff was not learning from adversity in their roles or growing in their positions at all. Provide the cover, but empower your employees to work their issues.

When I first put this principle into practice, I used to say, "Don't bring me a problem without a solution." I later modified it to add "or options" after an incident where someone on my staff took it a bit too literally. A team leader in the finance department didn't have a solution to a problem, so he never brought me the problem to address. I found out about the issue too late, when we could have been working on a solution together as a team.

Go to Where the Work Is Being Done

While a big part of your role as a leader may involve time in your office putting together dashboards, documents, and presentations, don't fall into the trap of getting glued to your office chair, like many managers do. Have you ever had a boss who never left his or her office? Never came out into your work area to check on you and your colleagues when there was something big going on? Think back to how you viewed this boss. Don't let that be you. Many managers who transition into leadership fall victim to the practice of "armchair leadership." Get out "into the field" often to see what is happening around you, how situations are handled, and to more directly interact with the staff. The best way to know what's truly going on in your organization is to speak directly to the people in it. Spend a few minutes seeing what's happening in the various areas. Give colleagues or staff updates on new things coming up or processes in the works. It's especially important to be visible during a crisis or difficult time. This helps to send a message that you value your staff's work and will support or lead them through whatever comes up.

While I served at the university, a major crisis occurred in the IT department with server maintenance. It wasn't something that they needed my help to fix, but I thought about how the staff had been up since two in the morning trying to fix hard drives, and decided to head over to the department to provide moral support. Understandably, when I arrived, there was a lot of commotion. Many were answering phones at the help desk, so I yelled over the crowd and thanked everyone. I also went into their temporary emergency-operations center and expressed my appreciation for their long hours and intense efforts to resolve the issues. I caught them doing good work and they knew it. They were tired but happy to be recognized and nodded back with a sense of satisfaction.

Counting on the Four Cs

My challenge to my employees involves what I call the Four Cs: candor, commitment, courage, and caring. I expect these qualities not only from myself as a leader, but also from those on my team.

Candor: You have to be able to admit mistakes and be honest about the true state of a situation. As I mentioned earlier, I don't like excuses or half-truths, so be a straight shooter at all times.

Commitment: I seek people who are committed to the mission of our organization. They will give the best of themselves to their tasks and activities. It is sometimes difficult to be part of a team or an important mission; I look for people who will not shy away from their duties.

Courage: Not only do I have to have courage to take on risks and more responsibility as a leader in my organization, but I also want to see courage from the employee's perspective. I expect employees to have the courage to express their opinions and to do the right thing for the right reasons.

Caring: I make an effort to get to know everyone in my organization on a personal level. Someone once told me, "People don't care how much you know until they know how much you care." I'm always cautious when I ask someone about themselves and they start basically giving me their résumé. I want to know what their passions are away from work, who the important family members are in their lives. I don't just want to hear about what they've done in their career. I call this kind of caring being "personally professional." I go out of my way to know spouses' and children's names to be able to ask my employees about their families when we get a moment to talk about something other than work. Caring leadership is contagious. When we as a team all care about each other—not only as coworkers, but also as people— I've found that we're better at getting the job done together.

When looking at your leadership style, think back to past interactions with colleagues or bosses. Did you exhibit the Four Cs? Are they part of your personality as a manager or leader already? If not, plan out small steps you can take to improve in these areas.

When bringing someone on to your team whom you've worked with before, did you notice if they exhibited the Four Cs in the workplace? When you speak to their references, be sure to ask about their work style.

You want to select staff who can grow into leaders, so identify if they have the Four Cs as well.

Eradicate Bad-Mouthing, Backstabbing, and Petty Attitudes— They're Disruptive to a Team

I've learned that it is best to nip rumors or negative comments as soon as you hear them. Don't tolerate gossip and backstabbing. Your team will engage less in these practices if they know you disapprove and won't participate. When you work around people who have negative attitudes toward the organization and leadership, it's hard to move forward in a professional manner. A poor emotional state among your team members will immediately decrease productivity, holding the team back from achieving goals. A better alternative is to create a welcoming and inclusive climate that fosters trust and allows employees to work in an emotionally safe environment.

Compass Check: What Will Your Leadership Style Be?

It's important to identify the traits that comprise your leadership style early on and communicate it to your team members often. When those around you understand your style of leadership, they will better understand the decisions you make and what is expected of them. This will help ensure that together, you form a more effective team, regardless of your field of work. Having a clearly defined style will also help you in your long-term career goals. When prospective future employers or managers are seeking a candidate to bring in to a leadership role on their team, you will stand out if you have a clearly defined leadership style that they can see aligning with the values and goals of their organization.

Visualize some great leaders you admire. Can you identify their styles of leadership? What traits or qualities do they have? Do you want to be the type of leader who gives commands to your team, or one who guides and teaches? Will they be intimidated by you, or feel comfortable coming to you with concerns and problems? Perhaps you have already developed some of the traits of your leadership style, but know that this is something that develops over time as you move into different roles. Feel free to adopt some of my leadership traits and of course add your own to your repertoire as you grow.

Management is efficiency in climbing the ladder of success; leadership determines whether the ladder is leaning against the right wall.
—Stephen Covey

V

RESOURCING TOWARD THE VISION

Aligning Money, People, and Time

When you're in a leadership position, it's not just about you—it's about building your team. For type A personalities and do-it-yourselfers, it can be challenging to empower the team and then step back to let them get the job done. As the leader you are there to facilitate and manage, while focusing your attention on higher-level strategy work instead of day-to-day operations.

After you've communicated your professional standards to your team, communicate the organization's shared vision and values. These are critical pieces of information your team will need to do their jobs effectively. One of the most important aspects of steering your team—and ultimately the organization—is to align resources with the vision.

Lack of efficiency and effectiveness can be the downfall of any good professional, but especially for the leader. How many times have you heard someone say of a politician that they are just not as "effective" as they used to be? Or that someone on a team in your organization is not as efficient in accomplishing their tasks as they once were, even if they have been given additional resources? It can be easy to get bogged down by minutiae, but a leader needs to be constantly working toward the bigger picture. It is the leader who is responsible for helping their team accomplish the overall goals of the organization. They needn't worry about the "small stuff" on a constant basis.

Effective leaders accomplish big-picture goals because they properly align the organizational resources with the mission that needs to be accomplished. Every organization or team has, to some degree, three main resources in common: funding, people, and time. How the organization's leaders manage these resources is the key to success. You can learn and put into place tools to help you utilize your most important resources in the best possible manner. This chapter includes tools and techniques that have been beneficial to me as a leader.

Funding

Once you understand the vision of your organization, you will put a plan into place for how to achieve it. But like anything in life, money will always be a factor. A leader must do what is best for the organization with the financial resources they have. Regardless of your line of work, I am sure you can immediately think of several things your team does on a daily basis that are impacted by money. I have found it valuable to share the key areas that I need to track with my fellow leaders and my team.

Tool: Metrics Dashboard

Think about your current position or role. What key areas impact your success or failure? Sales figures, total revenue, hours per project, etc. are some possibilities. What is your current method of tracking this data? If an executive in your organization needed to make a decision and wanted to see the latest metrics, could you immediately give him or her something tangible?

In both the military and at the university, I used what I refer to as a

"Metrics Dashboard," a group of charts showing the most important metrics I need to monitor for my department. Like the dashboard on your car, the critical data tracked in an informative way will let you know how you are doing and if there are warning signs before engine failure. Establishing and then using a Metrics Dashboard sends a message to your team and your management that you are staying on top of critical areas. It keeps you and your team focused on what is important and what needs to be accomplished. After all, "Doers do what checkers check!" The Metrics Dashboard reinforces transparency—there's no big "secret" about what elements should be important to subordinate teams. Employees also gain a better understanding of the big picture and how they contribute to the overall success.

How can you create your own Metrics Dashboard? First, think about what metrics need tracking, being careful to have both historical and forward-looking measurements. Jot down five elements. I recommend that your dashboard track no more than five critical areas. Any more than five could prove overwhelming, thus defeating the purpose. What metrics will you use to track critical areas—numbers, percentages, etc.? How often will you review the metrics? What is the standard or goal for the measurement? Is there an upper limit you don't want to exceed? Also decide if the dashboard is something that you will review regularly with your team, and if it is something that should be accessible to others in your organization who may not be directly on your team, but who can view it in order to help them make informed decisions.

People: Take Your Organization from Good to Great

You're already responsible for building a good team of people to work in your department, branch, etc. But have you thought about what will happen if someone leaves your team? What if you need to shuffle staff around? Many times when a person moves from management to leadership, they are used to hiring staff into the organization, but where they lack skill is in identifying and managing the talent pool that already exists in the organization. Jim Collins once said, "If we get the right people on the bus, the right people in the right seats, and the wrong people off the bus, then we'll figure out how to take it someplace great."[13] Sometimes that means promoting or shifting staff to other areas, but other times it can mean letting people go, a process that can be difficult in many organizations.

Performance Appraisals

Every person on your team should receive a performance appraisal or review of some kind from you at least once a year. Performance appraisals are a valuable tool to help identify strong and weak areas of your team members. Appraisals also provide staff with professional development opportunities and improvement plans. If your organization does not have a standard evaluation form, create one yourself. Always be sure to include comments to help the team member understand why you rated them a certain way, and give them examples of good or poor performance that stood out over the past year. Then discuss the appraisal or review with the team member in person. Don't just send it electronically or give them the report to read without any opportunity to discuss it with you and ask follow-up questions. Some organizations begin the process with an employee self-appraisal form, giving employees a chance to showcase their good work and perceived shortcomings. During counseling, leaders can get a sense of how the employee feels they are doing, and identify any areas of disconnect.

Exit Strategy

Don't be afraid to talk to your team members about their plans for the future during their performance appraisal or review. Do they feel they are getting what they need out of their position? Is it really something they are happy doing? Are they looking at retirement in the near future? It's not always a negative if someone decides to leave the organization. It may be beneficial to work in another department or a totally different company and then come back later better equipped for a new role. Or the role or mission the person was performing is antiquated due to technology or a business model change and that employee needs to consider a skill set change to stay relevant. These are difficult, yet crucial conversations that leaders must have to be honest with employees and for the good of the organization.

While you're at it, be sure to have your own exit strategy in mind. It's never too early to plan for the next move in your career. Most people do not stay at the same company—or even in the same industry—for their entire career. Keep an eye out for other opportunities or industries that would be a good fit for your skill set. Discuss your career aspirations with your boss, and ask for his or her help either getting professional development to shore up a skill set or finding opportunities for leadership. Network often with other professionals. Volunteer to work with nonprofit organizations or a committee at your child's school. Many leaders make the mistake of becoming too comfortable as they move "up the ranks" with a company, and stop updating their résumé and keeping their ear to the ground for other opportunities. Don't be caught unprepared should something happen with your position or your organization.

Tool: Career-Progression Planning

This is a collaborative tool to help you manage your staff and the positions in your organization. You will need to be prepared for how to shift your workforce to benefit the overall organization, and to deal with departures. Make a list of your staff and their current positions. Bring together a team of trusted leaders or those who have a vested interest in the future of the organization to serve on a career-progression planning board. The leaders who comprise the board will normally have firsthand experience of the employees being discussed and can add insight to future positions of responsibility. Next, identify job positions or roles in the organization that will become vacant in the near and long term. Consider who could be promoted or lateralled into the vacancy and where the incumbent could move to next. Can you name people who would be a logical progression to fill the empty slots that are created? Is there anyone who can be trained to fill the position?

Once you have a good draft, look for gaps in talent and start grooming employees to fill future vacancies. Keep your career-progression matrix updated. It's a living tool that needs to be tweaked as the situation changes. If a trusted employee suddenly gives notice, do you have a short list of qualified employees you can consider? If you need to let someone go because of consistent poor performance, prepare ahead of time by grooming individuals who can take on the role. Your goal is to ensure the needs of the organization are always met from a personnel perspective, and that the best people for each job are getting the training they need ahead of time, not after they've taken the position. Another benefit of having a career-progression board is that the employees who have a desire to move up in the organization will work harder to make themselves more valuable to the organization. Senior leaders also gain a visual tool of their bench strength and can then use the results to counsel employees on potential future roles. Additionally, crucial conversations will occur when the collaborative and transparent effort reveals certain employees have reached their potential or perhaps even stagnated. If a lateral move isn't feasible, then it may be time to discuss the employee's exit strategy.

Career-Progression Planning Tool[ii]

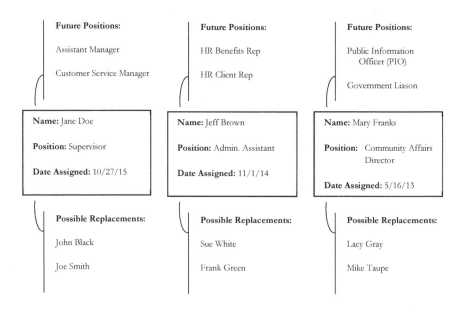

Future Positions:	Future Positions:	Future Positions:
Assistant Manager	HR Benefits Rep	Public Information Officer (PIO)
Customer Service Manager	HR Client Rep	Government Liason

Name: Jane Doe	Name: Jeff Brown	Name: Mary Franks
Position: Supervisor	Position: Admin. Assistant	Position: Community Affairs Director
Date Assigned: 10/27/15	Date Assigned: 11/1/14	Date Assigned: 5/16/13

Possible Replacements:	Possible Replacements:	Possible Replacements:
John Black	Sue White	Lacy Gray
Joe Smith	Frank Green	Mike Taupe

[ii] For a blank Career-Progression Planning Tool, see the Appendix.

Managing Your Time

Whether personal or professional, and regardless of your industry or organization, managing your time is an invaluable skill. This is also a skill that many would agree is the most difficult to master. Often our instinct tells us to take care of small, simple tasks first. If you're tackling the small projects first all the time, it can feel like you are accomplishing a lot because you may be crossing much off your to-do list. But are those the projects that will have the biggest impact? Are those the things you should be putting at the top of your list?

As a leader, you need to focus on tackling the large projects. Spend most of your time and effort on the most important aspects of your life. Stephen Covey calls these aspects "big rocks."[14] They could be career goals, your faith, time spent with your children or parents, mentoring others, or anything that is the most important for you to accomplish. Covey compares your time to a large jar, and illustrates how filling the jar first with big rocks gives you a chance to add in "little rocks" to maximize your remaining time. If you were to start by filling up your jar with all the small rocks in your life, you wouldn't have enough room at the end for the big, meaningful items.

Be prepared to become what I call "ruthlessly efficient." Most of us have a "to-do" list, but prioritizing the list and working efficiently to accomplish the most important tasks first is the pursuit of ruthless efficiency. Checking items off of a list may give us a sense of accomplishment in the short term, only to lead to frustration as you realize you're not getting closer to your life goals. It's the difference between working harder and working smarter. Look toward your True North for prioritizing your time. What are you working to achieve? Keep your eye on the "prize" you're envisioning.

You must also avoid distractions. What are those things that may pull your attention away from working toward your goal? If it's at the office, are there colleagues who engage in small talk too much and are a distraction? At home, are you distracted by a constant need to clean and organize rather than spending quality time with your spouse and children? Whatever it is that may be pulling you away from your main task, find a way to minimize or overcome the distraction. How can you do this?

Plan Ahead

Evaluate the tasks and events, both personal and professional, that you have ahead in your life and deliberately plan for them. Factor in deadlines, vacations, and unexpected issues. Essentially, begin scheduling yourself as far out from deadlines and events as you can to be sure you are prepared for them. If you have a big presentation for a conference due a few months out, plan out how much time you will need to complete your presentation, get peer feedback on it, revise it, then practice it all before the event. Set personal deadlines, and don't cut yourself any slack. Be sure to build in some padding for emergencies that may pop up in your personal life or with other work-related tasks. Challenge yourself to be looking at least a few months ahead. This can be difficult if your style has always been more "procrastination is king" than long-term planner, but you have to force yourself. Start small by planning a couple weeks out, and then build from there.

Set Aside Blocks of Time

You should literally schedule time on your calendar or agenda to work on your big projects. Block off time on your calendar when you are going to do research on a project, and hold yourself to it. Set aside days that are "working" or "planning" days, where you will not schedule any meetings, then stick to it. Scheduling your work in the same way you would schedule a meeting can be a good way to be sure you are making time in your schedule for critical tasks that otherwise could easily get pushed aside by small issues. Don't forget to schedule mental health breaks for yourself to unplug and recharge your batteries.

Use a Time Management System

Regardless of what technology devices you prefer, there are many options available now to help you create your schedule and manage the time you are dedicating to your personal and professional tasks. From calendar programs to apps to good old paper planners, there are myriad ways to map out your hours, days, and weeks. If your company already uses a calendar app, learn it and adopt it as your own. Speak to colleagues who are very organized with their time and see what works for them. Once you've selected a method, the key, of course, is to stick with it. Don't choose something cumbersome that takes you so long to update that you're spending more time on calendar management than you are doing actual tasks.

Delegate

Delegating is a struggle for any new leader. "If you want something done right, do it yourself" can no longer apply. You cannot do it all yourself, be it at home or in the office. Remember that you now need to be ruthlessly efficient with your time and energy. Consider the opportunity cost to the organization if you are working tasks that others can complete and learn from instead of tackling greater issues. If it's not absolutely critical that you yourself complete a task, assign it to someone else.

In some cases, you may even have to push back and create this awareness with your own supervisor. I once had a boss who asked for my involvement on a number of projects, but I knew I would be doing the greatest good for our organization if I passed off smaller projects to another person on our team. I could then focus my attention on the critical areas that my boss had asked me to be involved in.

Trust the team you have built to handle the tasks you assign to them. When you provide proper guidance, they will know what to do and know that if they have questions or concerns they should come back to you for further clarification.

Tool: Develop a Critical-Information Matrix (CIM)

A major subcomponent of managing time is prioritizing the flow of information. One tool I strongly recommend to help educate the organization on what's important to communicate is the Critical-Information Matrix (CIM). The CIM can guide you and your team in identifying what you want to hear and when you want to hear it. Communication is most efficient if leaders embrace a three-question litmus test for acting on information. The three questions I intuitively walk myself through are "What do I know?", "When did I know it?", and "What did I do with the information?" This matrix is a tool to help employees know "If I hear this it might be important, so whom do I tell and when?"

The CIM I've adapted originates from a matrix I came to appreciate in the military called the Commander's Critical-Information Requirements (CCIR). These requirements comprise information nuggets identified by the commander as being critical in facilitating timely information management and decision-making. The two key subcomponents are critical friendly-force information (what's happening with your workforce) and priority intelligence requirements (information you need to know to make immediate decisions in a crisis).

I adapted the matrix to suit nonmilitary communication needs after seeing that it could help educate and focus leaders in other professions. The CIM outlines, in a clear format, *what should be reported*, *when it should be reported*, and *who should get the information*. It includes crisis issues such as major errors or customer problems, data leaks, employee accidents/injuries, manmade or natural disasters, etc., as well as any degradation in service due to personnel issues or infrastructure breakdown. You can tailor the matrix to include information requirements important to your CEO or line of work. The reporting groups will also be determined by your organizational structure.[iii]

Here are examples of potential items that might comprise your organization's CIM:

- *Major damage to the facility.* What if there is severe flooding that causes damage to some of the physical space of your organization? Will you need to alert a few critical members of your leadership? Operations and facilities will need to know

---

[iii] For an example of the Critical-Information Matrix (CIM), see the Appendix.

the answers to these questions in order to either arrange for repair crews or assess the viability to use the space after the flooding. Timely communications may be required to notify staff or the public that the space is closed and cannot be used until repaired or cleaned. In the case of this type of issue, leaders of the organization should be alerted immediately.

- *Sensitive data is lost or compromised*: What if someone in the organization realizes that confidential customer information, such as credit-card data, has been compromised? This is something that needs to be shared with the appropriate parties immediately. You will not only want upper management to know, but also the communications and IT managers. The communications manager will need to issue a statement to consumers, as well as possibly answer media inquiries. The IT manager will need to immediately start investigating the source of the breach.

- *Media coverage of the organization or its staff*: If your organization is mentioned in the news—for either good or bad reasons— leadership team members will need to know. The communications manager is a priority to be kept informed, especially if reporters are intending to craft a follow-up story with the organization's response. It is always best to get in front of the story with full disclosure.

A large part of the matrix's value is in the collaboration it takes to create it. Bring the key stakeholders together as you work through the initial thumbnail for requirements. Use the sample CIM as a starting point for your company, adding or deleting items that may not be relevant. In my last position, after the first meeting with stakeholders to discuss actual information requirements, the reporting of safety incidents and infrastructure issues all increased exponentially. Information was being shared across silos, and dots were being connected like never before. It was powerful!

Compass Check: Get Your Toolbox Ready

As a leader, there will be many tools you will put into your toolbox while you grow and expand your career. Ensure you have tools that will help you align your available resources with the vision you are trying to achieve for yourself or your organization. Do they help you allocate your financial resources, save time, or put the best people in place? Regardless of your line of work, many of the tools apply universally, so carry your toolbox with you wherever you go. If you had told me when I was serving with the Georgia Army National Guard that years later I'd be in a critical position in higher education, I would have been skeptical. But the tools I learned and developed over the years in my time at West Point, the Guard, and my days in higher education have served me well and will continue to be transferable strategies and practices I will always use. Start creating or adding to your toolbox so you can add value in any role that moves you in the direction of your True North.

Leadership is the art of accomplishing more than the science of management says is possible.
—Gen. Colin Powell (Ret.)

VI

MOVING BEYOND MANAGEMENT

Transitioning to Leadership

There are studies in management showing that there is, in fact, some science behind being a good manager. But leadership may be viewed as more of an art than a science, and not all managers are able to master the art. Many people are great managers, but they will not all become great leaders—and that's not a bad thing. We need solid managers who will bring valuable contributions to their industries. Managers help to lead members of the team in the details of achieving the leader's vision.

The "genesis" of my leadership ability, coupled with a desire to be a servant leader, was cultivated and tested during my time at West Point. Prior to those four years, I was primarily focused on my education and getting accepted into West Point. My family could tell early on that I was destined for something other than a traditional career path. The steps I have taken since my youth have ultimately been driven by a special calling to lead and help others achieve.

Transitioning into a leader is a combination of changing how one thinks and adapting how one acts. Some people truly have the desire to lead, but perhaps not the ability to make the changes needed. A great quote from Benjamin Hooks, former director of the NAACP, comes to mind for me: "If you think you are leading and turn around to see no one following, then you are just taking a walk."[15] Professionals often think that they are functioning effectively as a leader, when their true function is actually as a manager. While the manager works toward the pursuit of predetermined objectives, the leader is striving to create enduring success for the organization.

The best leaders I have known had strong morals and demonstrated good qualities through their choices and actions, setting themselves apart from their colleagues. They show and give respect. They take risks. They always model the "gold standard" of leadership. The transition that takes place is a process whereby someone who has the innate skills of a leader makes the choice to go from being a good manager to being an effective leader. This does not happen overnight or subconsciously. It is a choice. For some it can take a few years, for others, decades. For me, it was a steady process over time of learning and developing my skills, habits, and beliefs. Regardless of the time the development takes, it all begins with the pillars of a person's Personal Leadership Philosophy (PLP). How do leaders stay motivated? Are they always focused on the mission at hand? Do they have good ethics and core values—honesty, loyalty, dedication?

If you're ready to throw yourself into the challenge of growing into a leader, here are my recommendations to help you transition from manager to leader.

Know Yourself First

It's time to do a little self-evaluating. You must acknowledge your flaws and give credit to your strengths. Identify your True North. What is your mission or purpose, and how will you grow in order to prepare for the next step in your career? Get ready for challenges, opposition, and different treatment by colleagues as you advance. Chinese general and military strategist Sun Tzu wrote in *The Art of War*, "An army may be likened to water, for just as flowing water avoids the heights and hastens to the lowlands, so an army avoids strength and strikes weakness." Others will want to hit you where you are weak or flawed. You have to be the one to identify your own weaknesses before someone else does and uses them as a means to hold you back.

In evaluating yourself, there are three areas you should pay special attention to:

- *Skill set strengths and weaknesses.* What is your capacity to move up into a leadership role? Do you lack certain skills, or have you not challenged yourself enough? If the issue is limited to your skills, there is an easy way to start correcting this flaw. Educate yourself! Get the assistance you need to turn your weaknesses into strengths. Otherwise, you are holding yourself back from growing into a leader. You can go back to school, take online courses, view webinars, or attend workshops and classes to get training in your weakest areas. I found it helpful to subscribe to specific professional journals, such as the *Chronicle of Higher Education,* to quickly benchmark best practices. Join professional associations in your field to network and find coaches. With the internet, there's really no excuse—you can find courses, videos, and articles in almost any area of interest.

When I accepted the position several years ago at a large Georgia university, I knew I was an effective leader and had many skills from my time in the Guard that translated into any line of work. But I did not have university-system experience and wanted to sharpen my skills. A university atmosphere is very different from the environment of the military. I talked to my supervisor about potential learning opportunities and was later nominated by my boss to participate in the University of Georgia System's Executive Leadership Institute (ELI). I anxiously accepted the challenge. ELI gave me the opportunity to meet and learn from leaders of other universities. It greatly enhanced my "toolbox" of skills to be better prepared in my new role. This preparation and extra training shortened my learning curve and provided me with a framework to start digging in quickly. Despite the different environment between the university and the military, I could see similarities in the culture and shared vision of the leaders. For example, both the military and higher education strive to be good stewards of the taxpayer's dollar, and they work to create a culture of safety from the top down.

- *Looking the part*: Are you mentally and physically up for the leadership challenge? It can be difficult to "look the part," especially for women, so put in the extra effort to put your best impression forward every day. This can mean several things. In the military, emphasis is placed on your physical fitness and strength. This often carries over into other industries or organizations as well. Do you look strong, healthy, and capable of stepping up to a challenge? Or do you look tired and out of shape? Do you carry yourself with confidence, exuding the feeling that you are prepared for challenges or action? If you feel you are losing focus on a topic, take a break and then reengage with more energy. Your head has to be in the game at all times. Dress professionally. It may sound cliché, but work at dressing for the roles or positions you want to achieve. Observe your office environment and then dress one level up. Otherwise your appearance may give the impression that you don't really care about being sharp. There are many professionals, male and female, who do not realize the importance of proper business attire. You want to enhance your professionalism, not detract from it. Be deliberate about your attire, hairstyle, and accessories. You won't have a second chance to make a good first impression.

- *Willingness to go all in*: Are you the type of person who shuts your eyes during a horror movie, or the type who leans in closer to the screen? If you hope to transition into a leadership role, get ready to take on things that you're afraid of with your eyes wide open. Instead of literal fears, like jumping out of a helicopter into a bay below, it's things like self-doubt or a fear of conflict that you will encounter. You now have to admit that there are things that scare you, and that it's time to confront them. Recognizing your fears will give you the power to control your response and expand outside of your comfort zone. Leadership is a decision to step up, a commitment to the team, a willingness to go all in.

I learned this lesson early in my career. While stationed at Fort McPherson, Georgia, the headquarters for the U.S. Army Forces Command, a large group of people gathered to protest the military operation called Desert Storm. I was a military police officer at the time, and my boss told me that they needed someone to tell the protestors that they could not block the gate, and he wanted to send me. He could have chosen a "big guy," but instead decided I was the best person for the job. He wanted someone nonthreatening who would have a calming influence on the crowd. More and more protestors were arriving, and I was about to be put in harm's way in front of the angry mob.

I was just twenty-eight years old and a young captain—nothing compared to the highly decorated generals we had on site—but I knew they had faith in me to get the job done, because failing would result in media and political consequences. If I did not handle the situation correctly, the crowd could become more riled and create a larger problem. Scared as I was, I resolved to just do the best I could. We worked out notes of what I would say. As a precautionary measure, my boss planned to have snipers on the roof in case it got bad.

When I exited through the front gate the protestors were screaming and chanting, "Baby killers, baby killers!" I was nervous but didn't want to show it. I had to act confident and encourage the crowd to quiet down and listen to me. Faced with angry people full of distrust, my mission was to create a sense of calm. I gave the speech I had rehearsed, telling the protestors they were trespassing on government property and that they needed to disband or they could be arrested. As I finished I scanned the crowd, looking to see if anyone had any weapons. Then a woman yelled out, "Do you have children?" My mind raced as I thought through whether to engage in conversation.

"Yes, I have two," I admitted. I realized right after I said it that it was possibly a bad idea to answer this woman.

Right away she shot back, asking me, "Well, how would you feel about your children going and fighting in this war?"

Now I don't remember exactly what I said, but it was something to the effect that I have two daughters, and I would set the example by being willing to fight in that war. I explained that we were only there to liberate the country, to push the Iraqi Army out of Kuwait and give the country back to its people.

By that time the crowd had actually calmed down and was quiet. They wanted to hear what I had to say. By talking to the woman as one mother to another, it seemed to change the whole dynamic of the crowd. I told them that although I did respect their right to protest, I needed them to please leave, and they ended up dispersing without further protest or violence. My heart was in my throat. I felt that maybe I had done something wrong by answering the woman's questions, but when I got back through the gate to safety, my boss said that I had done a fantastic job, even exceeding their expectations of the result. I did it scared, but I did it.

As a leader, you often have to step outside your comfort zone and take risks, and that can sometimes be scary. But having an ability to assess a situation quickly and adapt based on the circumstances can help keep your fears from getting in the way of your success in a situation. Be sure to look to the pillars of your PLP for internal guidance. The more important your goal is to you, the easier it will be to face things that scare or challenge you as you try to get there.

When Is It Okay to Show Emotions?

There will be times in your career and personal life when no matter how hard you try, you won't be able to control your emotions. It's natural. I remember one such time while I was with the National Guard . . .

I got down on the floor, in my neatly pressed uniform, and I held on to the devastated young woman who had lost her husband to an improvised explosive device (IED). His body, now resting in a flag-draped coffin, sat on a small airplane at a local airport. Although we were supposed to go out to meet the casket and present honors as it was taken off the plane, this devastated widow couldn't bring herself to do it, instead collapsing on the floor. I became afraid she might hyperventilate or worse, and by this point I couldn't help but cry with her. There were several soldiers from the unit present, along with leaders from the chain of command. We all wanted to comfort her but felt helpless in the moment. I made the decision to get down on the floor and lie next to her, hugging her tightly and eventually calming her down with the words I was whispering in her ear. I still tear up to this day recalling her torment. It was grueling to see her in such pain, and in the end, it was her choice to stay inside the airport waiting area. While I was with the pallbearers receiving his body, I could hear her screaming phrases to him and crying inside the building. My heart was breaking for her, yet I had to maintain a leader's composure and perform my mission of presenting honors to our soldier. In this circumstance, I did not care how I was judged by others. She was a comrade in arms, and I wasn't going to leave her fallen and alone.

I learned early on in my career when it was appropriate for someone in my position to show emotion and when it was not. Women, especially in a professional setting, are constantly watched for how they react under pressure. How many times have you heard someone condescendingly joking about how it "must be that time of the month" when a woman displays strong emotions? A woman's response may manifest in tears, while a man's tends to manifest in anger. But a woman's emotions can be a source of strength for others. For me, it goes back to being genuine. In the aforementioned story, I felt a connection with the grieving wife and I wanted her to know she wasn't suffering alone. The takeaway: let your empathy show when appropriate. Your toughest judge will be staring at you in the mirror.

Pay It Forward

What exactly does it mean to "pay it forward"? It's the practice where someone does something nice for you, and instead of paying that person back directly, you pass it on to another, thus helping someone else in need. As I think back over my life, there were many people who displayed an act of kindness that touched my heart and impacted my life's journey: the cross-country coach who recognized my grit and took the time to push me harder, the math teacher I had for all four years of high school who expected me early every morning with at least one problem I couldn't figure out, the woman at Fort Hood, Texas, who provided me with support through the first months of having a baby. The list goes on of those who have blessed my life with hugs, cards, encouraging words, or even constructive criticism.

As I matured as a leader, I realized that serving not only connects you with others, but it is an extension of your True North, your life's purpose. You may recall the third tenet of my PLP: "It is a greater gift to give than to receive." I resisted the calling to give back at first, knowing my plate was already full. Yet I felt so rewarded by each experience of doing a good deed that I started carving out the time to serve. I volunteered to teach the Sunday school kindergarten class when it was about to be cancelled for lack of a teacher. There were a dozen children in the class, but as a nonteacher, it felt like a hundred! It didn't take long for me to bond with each child and his or her parents. Instead of a faceless member of the church, I was now part of a faith family contributing to the next generation.

Take a look at how you can give back to the community by volunteering, perhaps at church or your child's school. Are there professional organizations you've put off joining? What can you do to make yourself a better leader and help those struggling in society? Identify activities you can participate in that you are passionate about. They do not have to relate directly to your job, but they should offer opportunities to help others while enhancing your professional development. For me, the work I do with veterans and future leaders helps me fulfill the servant component of my leadership style and gives me a sense that I am helping work toward a greater good in my community by sharing my time, skills, and knowledge with others. Paying it forward demonstrates your authenticity as a leader and shows you care about the larger community.

Create Strong Alliances

You may have heard the expression "It's lonely at the top." Well, this expression will begin to have more meaning for you once you take on a leadership role. It is critical to continuously work on forming professional alliances to help support you as you achieve the goals of your organization. Involve people with a shared vision for the organization. The people you want to build professional relationships with are those who want to step up and be part of something greater—the big picture. Value the diversity of thought that your professional peers can bring to your team, committee, or company; help empower them and work with them. You will be far more respected for helping your peers and working with them than if you only involve them to get the job done.

Oftentimes I volunteered to lead projects or special tasks that I wasn't asked to do, not because I was trying to make others in the organization look bad, but because I simply saw a gap in leadership or a need for the function. One example of this is my creating the information-requirements document highlighted in chapter V. I saw a disconnect in the flow of information up the chain and across silos. I knew it would be a contentious endeavor, but thought the benefit outweighed the cost of time and effort. By creating a collaborative process to address the communication flow of crucial information, team members saw an immediate value, and cross-talk began spontaneously even before the project was completed.

Remember these words from Arthur Ashe: "Success is a journey, not a destination. The doing is often more important than the outcome."[16] Recognize opportunities to work together with like-minded colleagues at your company. Together you will be more effective in achieving a goal or mission, which will go a long way in establishing yourself further as a leader whom others can look up to. One last caution: be careful of the toes you step on as you're climbing the ladder of success; you will most likely need to work with them when you reach the top.

Build a Network of Trusted Subordinates

You may remember the children's story by Hans Christian Andersen called "The Emperor's New Clothes." In this classic tale, two weavers promise to make an emperor an outfit out of a special material that cannot be seen by those who are unusually stupid or unfit for their office. Everyone pretends that they can see the material, even the emperor himself, who ends up parading through the streets of town naked, with all the townsfolk acting as if they can see the fabric so as not to appear stupid. Everyone keeps the charade going until a small child points out the obvious—the emperor is naked. Eventually all the townspeople are whispering to each other that, in fact, yes, the emperor is naked. But the emperor insists on keeping up the ruse and marches through the town with his head held high.

The lesson in this story? The emperor's staff had many opportunities to point out the obvious, but everyone, including the emperor himself, was afraid to be seen as lesser than or stupid, so they all kept up the lie. It took the honesty of a child to point out the obvious and get the adults to admit that there was no outfit at all.

Leaders must be brutally honest with themselves and recognize their blind spots. By being honest with yourself, you have the opportunity to surround yourself with people who can add value to your leadership and help overcome the blind spots. Regardless of your position or the industry you work in, you will quickly learn that many types of people surround you, some of whom will always say what you want to hear in order to stay in your good graces. Being surrounded by "yes" employees is dangerous to both you and the organization. Create a safe zone for a few trusted professionals to be able to tell you if your "baby is ugly."

While with the Georgia National Guard, we had an instance of having several hundred extra Meals, Ready to Eat (MREs) that had been ordered in anticipation of a difficult situation that did not come to pass. Since money had been spent to purchase the meals, it became a priority to consume the MREs before the expiration dates. A plan was put into place for soldiers to eat the MREs during the two weeks of annual training. We were so focused on not letting the MREs go to waste that we didn't consider the effect this could have on the service members. A subordinate officer, whom I had entrusted to let me know if my decisions were having an adverse impact, felt comfortable enough to speak to me about the concerns of the soldiers. He reminded me of the physical effect of eating almost nothing but MREs for an extended period—severe constipation. The news of having two MRE meals a day instead of one was causing an impact on overall morale.

Once I realized that there would be a negative effect on the soldiers, I decided that the extra MRE a day to substitute for a hot meal was not worth the financial advantages. The health and emotional wellness of the soldiers were far more important. We shifted priorities back to what was best for the soldiers, and made other arrangements for the extra MREs. As a servant leader, I take it as my personal responsibility to always weigh the morale of the team when considering the mission at hand. As a result of that soldier feeling empowered to report the complaints and concerns to me, I was able to reverse a decision that would have had unintended consequences.

Build a team of both peers and subordinates you trust to be honest with you. If you have been creating an environment where a difference of opinion is respected, this will be an easier process. Give them opportunities to have frank discussions with you about processes, decisions, actions in the workplace, and their views. As you build this network, stress to your team that you respect their opinions, that you trust their input, and that the purpose of the feedback process is not to give them free rein to criticize you, but to give you their honest assessment of the impact your decisions will have. It is important that this network be made up of peers who are on your level and subordinates you trust—both of whom you should have mutual respect for. To gain well-rounded input, be sure to select those individuals who have proven that they do not have the same views or ideas as you at all times. For this process to function best, you of course need to be ready and willing to take a bit of criticism and have your assumptions be challenged. You most definitely need to have tough skin, and if you don't already have it, this will get you there quickly.

Delivering Bad News to Your Boss

No one likes bad news, whether in their personal or professional life. But as a leader, you will sometimes have to be the "bearer of bad news." The key is in how you deliver the news and how you handle the situation that follows. I have adopted three techniques for delivering bad news:

1. **Duty to Warn:** There's a concept called "duty to warn," which is often cited in legal cases. It basically means that one party will be held liable for damages to the other party if they had the chance to warn the latter of a risk or hazard, but didn't. I firmly believe in the duty-to-warn principle. As a leader, it is going to often be your duty to warn your colleagues or your leadership of issues or flaws. You're essentially saving them from themselves. Like it or not, the "bad news" responsibility usually falls on the shoulders of leaders. Your true test will be having the courage to deliver the message.

2. **Go Ugly Early:** Bad news is not like a fine wine; it does not get better with age! Do not wait to share information on an issue; share it as soon as possible. Why "Go Ugly Early"? Sharing negative information early serves multiple purposes.

    a. It can help prevent rumors or false versions of a story.
    b. Letting your boss know of the situation will give you top cover if the planned solution goes wrong or doesn't work. It is better to be up front with the facts than to downplay it, or worse yet, sweep it under the rug.
    c. It can create productive awareness of a problem and bring more resources to the solution. Sharing negative news may make it seem like things are bad, but ultimately it can help create a safer environment. Being honest with information can calm fears or ease potential panic because the people around you feel better hearing timely and accurate information from a reliable source.

I recall an incident while working for the university where the school had a basketball doubleheader that was going to be live-streamed to ESPN. At the time, there was construction on the campus and power had been shut down, which inadvertently affected internet support for the center where the basketball games were going to be streamed within an hour. Somehow it wasn't communicated that there was going to be live-steaming that afternoon, and shortly before tip-off it was discovered that there wasn't enough power to properly support the streaming. Once the issue was identified, the response team worked quickly to fire up a generator to help with the needed power load. While the issue was in the process of being corrected, the team knew that they needed to alert their boss of the issue being dealt with, in case additional help was needed or other problems surfaced. The employee in charge of facilities on campus had to deliver the "bad news" to our boss and let him know what the issue was and how it was being resolved. It's not a conversation anyone wants to have, but it needed to take place and quickly. Even if he was not exactly to blame for the chain of events that led to the issue, the power-load problem fell under his purview—it was his duty to inform his manager. Bottom line: if something goes wrong and it falls under your department or responsibility, take ownership of the issue and deliver the news to your manager. Your courage to communicate the bad news while also attempting to solve the issue will give your manager a stronger sense of trust in your abilities.

3. **No Cant's, Just Costs:** No one likes to deliver bad news, but when you must, having a certain method of doing so will go a long way toward how the news is received. For the most part, supervisors prefer a "yes" answer when exploring ideas or working toward a goal. Instead of just telling your management or your team that something can't or won't be done, how about telling them what can be done and what the risks or costs will be?

During my command time in the Guard I had five brigade commanders and several primary staff officers. I remember one colonel in particular who wouldn't say no to an idea or mission. Instead he would say, "Sure, ma'am, we can do it. No cant's, just costs." This kind of response begs the question "What costs?" So I would have to ask him to explain what he meant. He'd tell me we could do something, but there would be financial consequences, be it more money spent, a realignment of budget, or something else having to be dropped because the troops can only accomplish so many tasks in their one drill weekend per month. He wasn't saying, "No, it can't be done," but informing me that there were costs and consequences that needed to be considered. It's an answer that most supervisors can't argue with or hold against you. By giving your management an alternative toward the solution, you are not automatically saying no to something or not wanting to work toward their vision. Rather, you're presenting a broader picture of the situation and contributing something of value.

No One Likes Bad News

When receiving bad news, keep this in mind: a leader's response to hearing bad news will directly impact how someone goes to that leader with bad news in the future. If you are given bad news, don't take it out on the messenger.

The phrase "Don't shoot the messenger" evolved in common language long ago through several origins, but the meaning is very relevant still today.[17] Greek biographer and essayist Plutarch wrote in his *Plutarch's Lives* that a messenger who gave notice of Lucullus's coming angered Tigranes and the messenger's head was cut off. Men were too scared to bring further information to him. This meant that he only received information from those who told him what he wanted to hear, instead of telling him the truth. Shakespeare also used a variation in *Antony and Cleopatra*. When the messenger gives the news that Antony has married another, she hits the messenger and threatens to gouge out his eyes. The messenger responds that he is only delivering the news.

When someone brings *you* bad news, do your best to not appear shocked or panicked. Try to not get angry with the person, instead controlling your voice and breathing to speak calmly. Ask questions rather than assume. Remember that it took courage on their part to come to you with something they knew could be stressful or upsetting, so be sure to thank them.

Don't Confuse Being Liked with Being Respected

There are many positives involved when you move up to higher-level positions. Unfortunately, moving up in the ranks can also come with some negatives. I have both personally experienced and witnessed that there will always be people ready to criticize or bring down someone enjoying professional success. They may try to find ways to bring negative attention to you or your actions, create false stories, or turn others against you. They may even try to take credit for the good work you have done. Do not confuse leadership with a popularity contest. General George Patton, while being criticized for being too hard on his men, once said, "Goddamnit, I'm not running for the Shah of Persia. There are no practice games in life. It's eat or be eaten, kill or be killed. I want my bunch to be in there first . . . They won't do it if I ask them nicely."[18] Some may view you in a negative light, but if you are treating people with respect and getting the job done, that is what will matter most for your organization long term.

As you make the mental transition into a leadership role, you must remember that your focus is on your job—your organization's mission—not whether you are "buddy buddy" with your staff. It's about being an effective leader who manages the team in a professional manner and works toward the goals at hand. A good leader will have some staff who "like" working for them, and some who don't. Often, it's a matter of holding people accountable, and most will rise to the occasion. The important thing is that if you are a good leader, your team will respect you for your vision and ability to improve the organization. Earn their respect and trust as their leader, not an invite to their barbecue.

I believe that one of the hardest parts of transitioning into a leadership role for women is coming to terms with the fact that not everyone is going to "like" you. Most women are innately programmed to seek approval, to be liked, to be seen as doing a good job. But in reality, there is rarely a leader who is universally liked and never criticized or judged. A mentor of mine in the Georgia Guard, Brigadier General Terrell Reddick, coined the phrase "Practice leadership, not likership." For years, a sign with that truism was posted at the entrance of the National Guard Training Center at Fort Stewart as a reminder and a challenge to leaders at every level.

If you are accustomed to hanging out with colleagues outside of work, be it going out for drinks or attending parties, and then you transition into the team's leader, you may need to assess and change some of those behaviors. Be careful not to put yourself into a situation that could be uncomfortable back at the office the next day, or if you have to discipline one of your coworkers. When it comes to interaction with employees outside of the workplace, be mindful of a double standard. Men's actions with their staff outside of the workplace are often held up in a different light than when a professional woman engages in the same activities.

What you think is innocent may be perceived differently or become fuel for negative gossip by someone with an ulterior agenda. Don't buy in to the logic of "What happens in Vegas, stays in Vegas." It doesn't, and it shouldn't. You're a leader twenty-four hours a day and seven days a week. Your actions on and off the clock define your character, integrity, and discipline. When you are a leader, others will hold you up as a role model. Don't make a bad choice in "Vegas" and expect that it will not catch up with you later. My advice is to always think about the kind of situation you are about to enter, and do the right thing for the right reason, even if no one is watching.

Watch Out for the "Queen Bee" Label

"Queen bee syndrome" was first defined by G. L. Staines, T. E. Jayaratne, and C. Tavris in 1973. It describes a woman in a position of authority who views or treats subordinates more critically if they are female.[19] Some women fear that they will not be taken seriously as a leader since they are female, so they overcompensate. They can be very assertive, may come off as "bossy," and could even make the mistake of putting down other women while trying to establish themselves as someone to be respected or even feared. In some cases, a "Queen Bee" may even do things that will hold other women back in order to gain favor with male superiors.

Fortunately, this syndrome has become less common in our modern workplace. Remember my story during Beast Barracks at West Point, of how the female upperclassman cadet grabbed the back of my head and yelled at me to do something about my hair? She was exhibiting this behavior. I vowed right then and there to never act in such a manner. I believe that women leaders should be mentoring others, helping both men and women move forward together in the professional environment. We can be our best advocate and resource for each other.

Road Rash . . . Tough Skin as a Leader

The journey to becoming an effective leader is not an easy one. It took me years to identify my fears, my flaws, and take steps to grow. Many times I have faced criticisms that were completely unwarranted and even hurtful. Be prepared to feel frustrated, annoyed, disappointed . . . but do not stew in those feelings. Let them motivate you to work harder to become a better leader and a better person. You will get scraped up, but the skin that suffers from road rash heals into thicker skin, making you tougher and better prepared for the next accident. Ernest Hemingway once said, "Courage is grace under pressure." How you handle difficult situations and negativity is a sign of your strength. Ignore unfair criticisms and focus on the critiques that are constructive and will help you grow.

Ask colleagues you trust to give you their honest opinions regarding your actions and mannerisms with peers both inside and outside the workplace. Reevaluate your work relationships and how you interact with others on your team. Are you too shy, too bossy? I'm a big proponent of the 360-degree survey tool that asks subordinates, peers, and superiors for feedback on your leadership style. Be prepared to hear things you don't like or agree with, but don't react defensively. You will get pointers that can help you grow.

One comment I received that made a difference for me suggested that I ask employees for feedback on how I'm doing. I thought I had already created an environment where it was okay for staff to give me feedback, but this comment took it a step further to actually *solicit* the feedback, positive or negative. Be grateful for any feedback, and then work on those areas where you're lacking the most. Sit back and assess yourself. Write down your limitations, your imperfections, and things that are holding you back, then start identifying ways to correct or improve in each area. Be sincere in your desire to expand your abilities and improve as a part of whatever team you're currently on.

Compass Check: Manager or Leader?

Are you ready to transition from a manager to a leader? It is not always an easy undertaking. It is a transformation of mind, body, and spirit. Your life, both personally and professionally, will shift as you make the transition, and you may find yourself taking actions or making decisions you might have avoided or overlooked in the past. You can expect to grow and adapt along the journey to becoming an authentic leader.

Remember to be patient. Don't get frustrated with yourself if you feel like you are not progressing quickly enough. Look for allies who can support you during the process, and always remember to help others along their journey in the same way that you would want assistance and support. Don't be disappointed with your organization if you feel they do not recognize your self-improvement efforts as fast as you'd like them to. When you're feeling overwhelmed or underappreciated, think of these words from Ted Engstrom: "The rewards for those who persevere far exceed the pain that must precede the victory."[20]

You only live life once, but if you do it right, once is enough.
—Mae West

VII

WHEN LIFE HAPPENS

Dealing with Life's Potholes

You're cruising along. You've found yourself in a good place: both your personal and professional lives are in sync, and in your comfort zone, you're not looking out for bumps ahead. You don't see that pothole in the road of life coming up. *Bam!* The car swerves and you're thrown out of your lane. If you're lucky, it's an easy adjustment to get back over. But what if your car hits a railing on the side of the road? Or worse, what if it goes into a ditch? Now you're in need of some serious repairs to get you back on your way.

Are you capable of foreseeing problems ahead? Throughout life, we all face problems, both big and small. What matters is how we respond to and resolve them.

Is Work-Life Balance Even Possible?

What makes you happy? This seemingly easy question is often hard to answer. Do you know what makes you happy? What is your purpose or driving force? The things that make you happy may be people, places, activities, or actual "things." Much in my life has brought me happiness, but occasionally one element of my life has taken up more of my time than another, and sometimes that one element has created more stress or frustration than another.

That's where "work-life balance" comes into play. You've heard the term before, but what does it really mean? Can you ever truly balance your personal life with your career? Most people—whether single or married, with or without children, working or staying at home—struggle to have aspects of their life balance out. My realistic answer on work-life balance is, it's not possible!

It took me years to realize that work-life *integration* is a better model. As you'll recall from my Personal Leadership Philosophy (PLP), it's more of an integration of mind, body, and soul—combining things in your life that bring you peace with the "must-dos" we all have. There will be times of stress, of being overloaded with work, or having your home life in turmoil. Then there will be times where all your puzzle pieces seem to fit together well for a while. That is the nature of life, especially for those who are putting in extra effort to work toward a leadership role in their career. Whether you are a woman or a man, I promise you that at some time in your career you will struggle with this concept of balance and integration.

I have learned many lessons about trying to create work-life integration. Some came easily, while others felt like an uphill battle with bruises suffered along the way. By sharing some of my personal-life experiences in this chapter, it is my hope to inspire you, no matter what you're going through, to find happiness and inner peace.

Women: Embrace Your "Flaws"

Both women and men are often guilty of pressuring themselves to be perfect and to "do it all." This may be caused by pressure from family, colleagues, friends, or images portrayed by modern-day media, but whatever the cause, that pressure can be a limiting issue, especially for women. It's natural for women to be more sensitive and caring toward those around them, to take criticism more personally, to wear their emotions on their sleeves . . . along with a host of other traits that some would call "feminine specific." The mistake is to allow these characteristics to be labeled as shortcomings, and to see them as "flaws."

Instead, women should look to these aspects of their personality as strengths. The things that make us different from our male counterparts can be advantageous. If you are very sensitive to the needs of those around you, you may be viewed as a more approachable and caring boss or mentor than a male colleague. If you take your work personally and don't take criticism well, you may work extra hard on projects to get them right. If you can sometimes be emotional, learn to employ those emotions to create powerful, moving moments when conveying your vision or debating an issue you care about deeply.

Beware of Making Career Decisions Based on Relationships

Several times in my career I made a decision or chose a path because of my relationship at that time. One can become conflicted very early. However, think twice before making career decisions based on your significant other's goals and aspirations. Be careful not to subjugate your dreams and happiness to conform to their life preferences. There are compromises that have to be made to build a life together, especially when children are involved. Make sure to voice your desires and not always be the one to put your aspirations on the back burner. In the long term, you will have a stronger relationship if both members of the team are accomplishing their goals together, rather than one at the expense of the other. It is possible, but it takes frank conversations.

I was young and in love when my world was shattered because I didn't follow this advice. As a "firstie," or senior, at West Point, I fell madly in love with a fellow classmate. He was perfect in my eyes—handsome, witty, smart, and adventurous. We had great chemistry and I trusted him, even to the point of letting him certify me to become scuba-diving PADI qualified. We met each other's parents, and were soon engaged to be wed after graduation.

We knew that if we wanted to be assigned together for our first tour, we would have to pick the same military-officer branch and then accept the base location that could accommodate two lieutenants. My fiancé had strong aspirations about becoming a military police officer and going to the FBI Academy and perhaps law school. I, on the other hand, hadn't considered law enforcement, preferring to go into the corps of engineers and put my engineering education to use. While I admired crime-fighting heroes, I never fashioned myself as a police officer, but in the end, I put my goals aside so we could have a better chance of being stationed together and agreed to select military police as my branch. The Army assigned us both to move to Fort Hood, Texas, after graduation. For a while, everything went as planned. Graduation loomed two months away as I found the perfect wedding dress and my mom prepared to drop the invitations in the mail.

Then he dropped the bombshell.

Maybe things moved too quickly, perhaps he got cold feet, or maybe he realized he loved a former girlfriend more than me. No matter the case, I returned his ring and cancelled the wedding. So there I was, set to go Fort Hood to be with him and on to a career that I didn't really want. The course was set, and not wanting to accept defeat, I made a choice to stay positive and embrace my new path. Looking back, I don't regret having chosen military police. I had the opportunity to serve with not just patriotic men and women, but with those who dedicated their lives to an even higher calling. The MP motto, after all, is to "protect, assist, and defend."

Take Your Time When Committing to "Forever"

Four months after the breakup, I met my now ex-husband at the Military Police Officer Basic Course at Fort McClellan, Alabama. We sat next to each other and shared a desk in class, eventually becoming friends after I accidentally slammed his fingers in the desk drawer! Over the four-month course, we grew very close. Although we shared many of the same interests, had easy conversations, and enjoyed each other's company, it didn't make sense to think long term. He thought he was being assigned to a 1st Cavalry Division unit in Germany, while I was going to Fort Hood, Texas. We were both surprised and happy to discover that he was actually being assigned to the 1st Cavalry unit at Fort Hood. It seemed like fate was pulling us together.

Once we arrived at Fort Hood, we leaned on each other for support and our love began to grow. We dated for six months before becoming engaged, setting the wedding date for early August of the same year. Looking back, I don't know why we rushed into marriage. For me, it just seemed like the natural thing to do. I had watched many of my classmates get married right after graduation with fairy-tale weddings, and even though I was only twenty-two, somehow I felt I was behind on an artificial timeline society had created. In retrospect, we should have courted longer, gotten to know each other better, and had hard philosophical discussions on ambitions, values, financial goals, religion, and child-rearing. But we were in love and waved away any differences we may have detected, assuming we could work it out. I pictured myself growing old with this man, and for me, that's all that mattered.

If you're currently single or divorced and haven't found "the one" yet, be mindful of the pressure to settle down. I believe it will happen when it's meant to happen. Until then, you'll need to ignore comments and questions from family, friends, and colleagues about why you're not married yet. I have seen too many people marry young (myself included), only to realize later on as careers progress that the person they rushed to marry was not willing to make the sacrifices required for a successful marriage.

Pregnancy Bias in the Workplace

In 1985, less than a year after we married, I became pregnant with my first child. I was an MP in a combat unit, and we would alternate between "white hat" police patrolling, which is where we served as the police force on the base and responded to incidents, and rear-area security missions in support of combat units training at Fort Hood. While five months pregnant with my daughter, I strapped on my load-bearing equipment, grabbed my rucksack, and headed out to the field with my platoon. As the platoon leader, I wanted to be sure to set the right example. Since I wasn't showing all that much, I didn't think anything of gearing up while pregnant. After all, I was still running with the platoon each morning, and I felt great.

After being in the field for a few days, I got a call from my commander to come back in to the unit headquarters. He told me that one of my peers had miscarried a week prior from training during field duty, and what was I doing? He informed me that a new directive had been passed down through the chain of command that pregnant soldiers weren't allowed to perform field duty. I hadn't considered being restricted from field duty, and if I couldn't lead from the front, then as much as it pained me, I had to ask for reassignment for the good of the unit. It was a difficult conversation to have with my boss, the company commander, but he understood and worked with me on the reassignment to another leadership position within the larger organization.

I hadn't really thought about the implications of being pregnant. I just knew that I wanted to start a family. I was taken out of a unit that I loved and placed into the law-enforcement activity, which turned out to be a wonderful experience. I learned a great deal more about the management of training and operations and doing all the behind-the-scenes planning.

Three years later while still on active duty, I had an opportunity to compete for company commander of the military police unit at Fort McPherson, Georgia, a position a woman had never held. This was to be a difficult role, because not only are you the leader of 250 soldiers who are military police, but you're also the commander of troops, leading the parades every month for the Forces Command four-star general. This involved directing the marching of 200 soldiers, calling out the commands to the soldiers, the salute battery to fire the cannons, and the band, all with several hundred spectators in front of you. Meanwhile, you also need to concentrate on the saber you're holding and saluting with. Fortunately, I had to perform similar marching drills at West Point, so although it was a high-pressure position, I was confident I had the leadership and skill set to be successful.

During the interview for the command position, at the time being eight months pregnant with my second child, I was asked several questions by the colonel who was the garrison commander. The interview was conducted in a sitting area consisting of two leather chairs separated by a small table with a lamp. To make eye contact with the colonel, I had to keep leaning forward during the interview, and being far along in my pregnancy, doing so was painful. One question that struck me was: "Can you lose the weight?" I remember sitting there and thinking, *Why would he even ask me that? Do you ask the guys that, too?* Yes, I was eight months pregnant, but I'd only gained twenty-five pounds. I was running every day until the five-month mark! He wanted to know that I would be able to get back into shape before I became the company commander, as there was a physical component to the position. I assured him that I would lose the weight, be back in shape, and be the best company commander he'd ever had. Six months later, I was ready for my change of command and I took over. Years after this assignment, that colonel continued to follow my career. I didn't disappoint.

Despite all the positions I have held and the recognitions I have received, being a mother is what I'm most proud of in my life. I became pregnant within the first year of my marriage, and while I'm glad now that I started early, I can also argue for waiting until career and finances are more stable. Know that if you are planning on becoming a working mother someday, it won't be easy. Even though many strides have been made since my own pregnancy, a bias still remains. Women will continue to have babies and be forced to deal with the perceptions that men have about women being pregnant in the workplace. Should you become pregnant, don't fall victim to overcompensating for those perceptions. The last thing you want to do is overwork or overstress yourself and jeopardize the health of the baby to try to prove coworkers wrong. Let them think whatever they want. Make the decisions and take the actions that are best for you. It's important to lean on your core values. Never let anyone make you feel weak. Carrying a child is one of the most difficult things a person can put their body through. Don't let anything stop you. You don't want to look back on your life after it's too late and have regrets.

Falling Asleep at the Wheel Is a "Wake-Up Call"

It once took a scary incident for me to realize how much I was pushing myself at work and at home to try to be perfect in both areas. In 1991 I was a wife, the mother of a two-year-old and a five-year-old, and the first female commander of troops. I was constantly trying to prove myself, to break the glass ceiling for other women, and there was a lot of pressure on me—much of it self-inflicted. I was up half the night with my two kids, going in to work early at 5:30 a.m. to do physical training with the troops at reveille, getting home late, then starting the routine all over again. This all changed one morning when I received a literal "wake-up call." I was getting off of a highway ramp to go to Fort McPherson when I fell asleep and went off the road, hitting alert strips. Luckily, those woke me up and I quickly corrected. I didn't get into an accident, but I realized that I had exposed myself to serious injury. Was it worth it? I started to reexamine my life, my ambitions, and my drive to do it all. It became apparent it was all too much.

Choosing Family over Career

By my eighth year, I was on a fast track in my career, getting great evaluations. I had been accepted at Georgia Tech to earn a master's degree in industrial engineering, but the Army had other plans for me. They needed MPs with engineering backgrounds to serve in an alternate area called Nuclear Weapons Effects. It meant I would be moved to someplace like Fort Leavenworth, Kansas, or Korea, and that I would need to move every two years. By this time my husband, children, and I had been living in Georgia for four years and owned a home. My husband was reluctant to follow me around—his family was here and this was home. I realized that I was going to have to give up my active-duty military career. I had busted my rear end for eight years, and I knew we were going to have to sacrifice by moving around, but *I loved being in the Army. I loved being a leader.* It pained me, but for the sake of stability I made the decision that I would end my active-duty service—a decision I would come to regret. I didn't realize at the time how much it would impact my future.

From Combat Boots to High Heels

At the time that I decided to leave the Army, I had been working on getting a human-resources degree through Georgia State University. A fellow West Point grad suggested that I interview the HR folks at his employer, a major bank, to help me with some coursework. It turned out they interviewed me, and offered to place me into a management-associate training program that fast-tracks the candidates over a one-year period to prepare them for a leadership position within the bank. I was getting out of the Army, needed a job, and so I accepted the offer.

It was a new challenge, but I enjoyed it. I also joined the Georgia National Guard on a part-time basis, doing one weekend a month while working for the bank. I was still able to serve my country, be in uniform, and be a leader . . . but I began to feel depressed. Being a civilian was very different from the Army. I enjoyed being able to wear dresses to work and look more feminine, but also missed the esprit de corps of the military.

After completing the training program, I ended up in mortgage lending, and luckily, there was an office in my hometown. I did the work for a year, but grew unhappy. I thought not having a commute would make me happy, but it only allowed me to work longer hours. I became more and more depressed. I felt no purpose or meaning in the work I was doing. It got to the point that my husband even told me I should quit because I was just miserable—and making everyone around me miserable. But like a good soldier, I refused to quit, not wanting to give up on the mission.

My job shifted to doing loan refinancing, but I had no experience in it. I was making mistakes and angering people. The job was demanding. I began working later and later, even working weekends to keep up with the workload. With some of the mistakes I made, they ended up taking money out of my paycheck to make up the difference in a loan. Since I was already making less than I had been in the Army, this was a big blow. Finally, I realized it was time to get out—this job didn't align with my values. I had to do a gut check and recalibrate.

My advice for anyone changing careers is to figure out what your values are and stick with them. Don't try to be someone you aren't. I thought I would enjoy being a banker or a mortgage officer, but the work just didn't align with me being a servant leader. I wanted to help people, but my job was to get those people to pay more than they should for a home and make them feel good about it. I sat at church on Sundays among those who trusted me to get them the best deal possible, and I felt terrible about what I was doing in my job. It didn't align with my personal values and certainly wasn't helping me to stay true to myself.

Breaking Down

I was unhappy with how my career had progressed and was not feeling that I was serving a greater purpose. My husband was there to "help" with raising our two children, but I had to ask him for help each time I needed it. I felt like I was nagging him, and didn't like the person I was becoming. Our seven-year marriage was strained, and we were both becoming dissatisfied with its state. But I was committed to making things work. Even though I was having doubts, I did not believe in divorce. I told myself that I still loved this man and I could see this crisis through. I began to feel totally trapped by my own desire to keep things together.

After a big blowout with my husband, the likes of which rarely ever happened, I balled myself up on the bathroom floor, completely and totally depressed. We started talking about splitting up because we had to face the fact that things weren't working anymore. My husband didn't know how to handle the situation, so he reached out to my father for help. He put the telephone in the bathroom and told me my father was on the phone. My family didn't really know what was going on. They knew that I was unhappy, but did not understand the full extent of my mental state. My dad offered to come down the next day, but also told me that all married couples have problems. The talk with my dad helped me realize that I needed to get some counseling.

I have a tendency to seek perfection. I wanted to have the perfectly clean house, the empty laundry baskets, the ability to serve dinner to my family every night—the good wife, the good mommy, and the good worker. In short, a mission impossible. I began to realize through counseling that I needed to figure out what was most important in my life.

I had to learn to let go of some things, and not stress if the floor didn't get washed one weekend or if I skipped laundry once in a while. I was shown that I—not my husband—was my worst enemy. He wanted me to be happy, but to me, being happy was doing it all and doing it right, which I couldn't do. This is a mistake too many women make. As they say, "Perfect is the enemy of good."

My husband and I eventually worked our way out of the bad place we were in. After leaving the mortgage job, I ended up getting hired by the Georgia Army National Guard as a project officer for the 1996 Olympics serving on the Security and Intelligence Subcommittee. It was wonderful to be back in uniform, using my law-enforcement skill set and doing something that I loved—serving the greater good. My compass was once again aligned on my core values.

Dumbing Yourself Down

My career with the Guard began to really pick up, and I felt that things were finally going well for me. My husband was also serving in the Guard and it was a nice common ground for us. As time wore on over the years, things changed. Instead of being proud of me and what I was doing, resentment began to seep in. I suspect that he wanted to be seen as the man in the family, and worried about how he was perceived with his wife moving up the ranks in the Guard. I started to feel that I needed to dumb myself down and slow down my career advancement. But what good would that do me or the organization? Women sometimes fall into this trap. We think that if we dumb ourselves down, or don't talk about the things we have accomplished, that it will make the men around us feel less threatened. That's wrong, but it took me some time to figure that out.

After more than twenty years of marriage, I began to see warning signs that things were not going to work out. I had figured out that he had other interests outside of our marriage. He gave up on marital counseling after barely participating in the sessions we did attend. The harder I tried to pull him in, the more he resisted. But I was not going to let myself get depressed again. I had grown as a leader and had learned to lead myself through my own personal crises. I went back to the counselor I had seen years before, when I had struggled with depression. The counselor helped me to see that I needed to find a balance between career Maria and wife Maria. She asked me if I thought my husband would love me more if I gave up on a career and stayed home. I realized that no, he wouldn't love me any greater. If I resigned from the Guard, I knew it would not change the state of my marriage; it would only make me miserable because I would not be fulfilling my purpose. My career was part of my being, and I could not give that up with the expectation that he would suddenly love me more. If I appeased him, it would destroy me. Yet I couldn't bring myself to let go of my marriage.

After a few months, the counselor abruptly ended our sessions. One day she said to me, "I can't help you anymore." She told me that a marriage is like a boat and that it takes two people to row the boat. If I'm the only one rowing, then I would just continue to spiral down into a deeper abyss. I needed to snap out of denial and face the fact that I was alone in the marriage. The ball was in my court and I had to make the decision on what to do next. It's not what I wanted to hear. As many of us often do, I wanted a magic solution.

Recognizing the End

The last five years of marriage were rough. The fault was equally shared. We were both stubborn by refusing to acknowledge that a serious course correction was required. At the end of 2009, I finally made the decision that it was time for a divorce and contacted an attorney. It turned out my husband had already reached out to the same attorney. I was shocked—he hadn't brought up divorce at all.

In the spring of 2010, I couldn't endure the suffocating environment anymore and moved out with my youngest daughter. The divorce was draining my emotional well-being, as well as my bank account. During the divorce process, my attorney suggested that I was being too accommodating with the terms and too generous with splitting our savings. Even though my ex had wanted the divorce, I wanted to be fair.

The divorce was complete in September of 2010. It had been a grueling and ugly year, but I survived. Afterward, the presiding judge for the divorce provided me with some sage advice. He said, "The best revenge is living a good and happy life!" Even so, divorce is hard and closure comes slowly, if ever.

What may help in a situation such as this is to be certain your side is fairly portrayed and represented, whether in a personal matter or workplace issue. Following this path will allow you some semblance of closure and will help you to seek out your good and happy life.

If you have children with your ex, look out for them, as well. You are grieving or even feeling depressed, but they are feeling something, too. During the course of a separation or divorce, children may try to do things to "help" the situation, possibly even hoping to repair their parents' relationship. Or they may not understand at all what is happening and be frightened and confused. I made sure to comfort my children and try to help them work through their feelings about their father and our family splitting up. I could tell that one of my daughters needed extra support. I asked her if she wanted to talk to someone else about her feelings. She agreed and went through counseling to work through the emotions she was struggling with. She needed to find her own voice with her father and not feel the guilt or blame for her parents' decision. Children don't get a vote in the divorce, but the impact has a profound, often untold impact on their lives. I may have been working full time and completely stressed by financial concerns and the divorce proceedings, but my children remained my first priority.

Taking a Hard Look at My Marriage . . . and Myself

After the divorce, I began to explore the process of an annulment through the Catholic Church. My faith has always been an integral part of my life, and now more than ever I needed healing and understanding. I had to take a very hard look at our relationship, how it began, why we got married, and if we were prepared to enter into the sacrament of marriage . . . all after twenty-six years of marriage.

For two years, the request for annulment was reviewed and investigated. In the end, the annulment was granted and the Catholic Church declared the marriage null and void, allowing me to fully participate in the holy sacraments. This process, although lengthy, helped me to come to terms with what had been wrong in our marriage. It also made me understand I needed to forgive and show more compassion. Afterward, I wrote my ex-husband to thank him for the good times we had shared, the beautiful children we had brought into the world, and I mailed it to him after he remarried. I needed to let go, to move on, to forgive.

Your Most Important Career Decision

Sheryl Sandberg, author of the acclaimed book *Lean In,* once said, "The most important career choice you'll make is who you marry. I have an awesome husband, and we're 50/50."[21] Sandberg, the chief operating officer of Facebook, whose husband, David Goldberg, passed away in 2015, credited her husband for being a strong support system for her and helping her to achieve a work-life balance that worked for them. That's right—one of today's most respected businesswomen says her most important career decision was her spouse. Not her degree, her mentors, or her résumé, but the person she married. The person you build your life with and go home to every day is more important to your career than you may realize. Pick someone who will be happy for you and proud of you regardless of what is going on with his or her own career, someone who encourages your growth and increased success, someone who shares the workload at home or even steps it up a notch when things get more hectic for you work-wise.

Compass Check: Facing Your Adversity Head On

Throughout your life you may face times of great personal struggles, and they may even come at moments when you're also in the midst of professional adversity. I have always tried to stay true to myself and my leadership principles in times of struggle. It took me time to get to that point. Gone are the days of the thirty-year-old crying on the bathroom floor or the young mother falling asleep at the wheel. I now pace myself.

If you are facing personal challenges, one of the most critical things you can do is acknowledge that you need help. Unfortunately, many people don't get to that point. It's common to be in denial; I certainly was for many years in my marriage. I would imagine it's like being addicted to a substance. Until *you* decide that you are addicted and need help, there's no one that can help you. Once you make a decision to get help, there are lots of resources, whether to help you cope with the loss of a loved one, the end of a marriage, stress on the job, or an addiction. The amount of compassionate help and affordable resources available will amaze you.

It's also common—and easy—to blame another person. But is the issue really all their fault? Do you share any of the blame? This is where a counselor or a process like the annulment I went through can help give you a new perspective. A counselor can serve as an unbiased third party to help you look at your struggles in a new way.

Don't suffer in silence. You have to work through the problems you're facing. One definition of insanity is doing the same thing over and over and expecting new results. Nothing's going to change until you change your mind and realize the power you have right now to get new results. Face your adversity and embrace it.

Face reality as it is, not as it was or as you wish it to be.
—Jack Welch

VIII

WHAT DOESN'T
KILL YOU...

Emerging Stronger after Workplace Crises

It is a given that we will all encounter adversity. How we respond to it is what matters. West Point was a good start for preparing myself for tough situations. But after years of service in the military, I eventually found myself in a situation that no amount of drills or training could prepare me for. In September of 2011, after twenty-eight years of exemplary service, I was told that the governor had decided to replace me as the assistant adjutant general of the Georgia Army National Guard. My military career, my livelihood as a single mom, came to an abrupt halt. Any aspirations to compete for my boss's position as the adjutant general (TAG) of the Georgia Department of Defense were dashed. I had cracked the glass ceiling, only to be denied totally shattering it.

I had a hint it was coming a short time before, when my office received a call from the governor's chief of staff requesting a meeting with me. Not too long before that call, my boss had received a similar summons and was told he was being replaced. Georgia state law mandates that you can't hold the position of adjutant general once you reach the age of sixty-five. My boss was turning sixty-five that year, so the replacement was not unexpected. I, on the other hand, was fifty, and had successfully led the eleven thousand men and women of the Georgia Army Guard—more than three-fourths of the entire group—through a tumultuous war-fighting period for over four years. I expected to at least be allowed to continue in my current position to facilitate a smooth transition with the new adjutant general, but unfortunately that did not happen.

Run an Emotional Rehearsal

When my presence was requested at the state capitol, I knew that something unpleasant might happen. The day before the meeting, I ran through various scenarios and conducted an "emotional rehearsal" of sorts. In the military, we create multiple scenarios with a "most likely" and "least probable" spectrum of outcomes. I'm a disciple of planning for the worst but hoping for the best. I tell myself, "It might be this," or "They may say that," playing out any number of possible outcomes to the meeting.

If you have a hint that you are headed in to a difficult situation, you can prepare yourself ahead of time to better manage your emotions during the situation. The goal is to never let them see you sweat. Mentally running through something ahead of time lets you feel the emotions before they happen, allowing you to then listen better and be more present during the actual situation. If you're sad, cry it out ahead of time. Angry? Go ahead and vent the day before with your spouse or a friend. Ask for honest feedback on your body language and facial expressions. Practice in front of a mirror, or even take a selfie! Don't wait until you get to the event to start feeling the emotion; you need to feel it and work through it beforehand.

When it's time, put on your game-day face. Compartmentalize and focus. It's very difficult, and it's taken me years of practice to be able to refocus my mind when my heart is racing with anxiety. Know your personal signs that can alert you to when your emotions may rise—your heart starts beating faster, your palms get sweaty, or you feel the blood rushing to your face. When I feel any of these signs beginning to impact me, I start calming myself down by taking a breath, relaxing my body position, and refocusing on what I'm doing.

Think back to an emotional situation you wish you had handled better. What would you do differently? Make a mental note and try this technique in your next highly charged situation. It takes practice.

It's Not Personal, It's Just Politics

When I met with the governor's chief of staff, there were five other men in the meeting. I felt as if I were on trial. The chief of staff asked me three questions during the meeting: *What makes you qualified to be the commanding general of the Georgia Guard? What exactly do you do every day? What have you accomplished as the commanding general?* I made the assumption that he and the other men in the room had little knowledge of the Guard, let alone military service, so I kept it simple.

Starting with my credentials, I outlined my education, beginning with graduating from the nation's premier leadership school, the United States Military Academy at West Point. I continued with my active-duty service over eight years, including being a platoon leader and an MP company commander, being branch-qualified as both a military police and military intelligence officer, commanding an MI battalion, earning two master's degrees, graduating from the U.S. Army War College, serving as the G1 director of personnel, and then as chief of staff before assuming duties as the commander. Not only was I fully qualified to become a general, but I had received both a U.S. Senate confirmation and White House approval.

I explained that every day is different based on the mission and priorities. I took the chief of staff through the number of important advances and programs I had instituted during my tenure, including the Georgia Guard going from middle of the pack to number one in both medical and dental readiness in the nation; the two new brigades I fought to bring to our state, which added another 1,200 jobs and more opportunity for advancement; the vast improvement in soldier training with the establishment of the premobilization training site at Fort Stewart; doubling the Yellow Ribbon Program and the size of the Chaplain Corps to address the extreme stress on families during multiple deployments; and many other accomplishments designed to improve not only the readiness of the Guard as an organization, but the lives of the soldiers and families as well.

The chief of staff took the time to carefully listen to my responses, even mentioning that I certainly had a distinguished career. But in the end, my responses made no difference in what he was going to say. It didn't matter what my qualifications were or the accomplishments I had achieved. It wasn't about me or the organization; it was about a different agenda, something that was foreign to me as a servant leader. I was, in essence, being erased. He was careful to stress that I was not being fired, that I was being replaced. "Big difference," he said. But it felt like I had just been put through a mock trial followed by exile. To add insult to injury, I would later be uninvited by the new leadership to attend any homecoming events for troops I had sent off to war.

Before I departed the room, I intentionally shook the hand of each gentleman and looked them squarely in the eyes. I sensed empathy in half of the eyes that I looked into—they knew what was transpiring, and they knew it was wrong. Yet there was nothing they were willing to do about it. It's remarkable how people will flock to you when you have power and can help their agendas, but when circumstances reverse, you hear crickets chirping above the silence of nonexistent protest. Once an optimist concerning human nature, I now find myself jaded by the self-serving and hypocritical behavior I have witnessed firsthand, multiple times.

Having had faith in the system, I found myself caught totally off guard by the three-week notice of replacement. When I knew my boss, the TAG, was on the way out, I had thought that I would have the chance to compete for his job, or at least stay in my current position. I even had received signals from the new TAG that I would be staying when he told me at a luncheon that he was "looking forward to working with me." I suddenly found myself with no résumé, no civilian business cards, and no exit strategy. In addition, two of my daughters were living with me and I was now a single mom. I had no idea what I was going to do next. After twenty-eight years of military service with twenty in the Georgia Guard, I realized how much of my life was invested and entangled in not only my career, but the community of men and women I had grown to respect and love. I didn't want to do anything else but serve. The work that I was doing was perfectly aligned with my PLP. My mind was reeling, my heart was broken, my faith was being tested—I had just been severed from something that I'd given my whole adult life to. I scoured my mind to determine where the fault lay.

Initially I blamed myself, thinking that maybe there was something else I could have done to prevent this horrible outcome. But I came to realize that no, this wasn't about me; this was about the use of raw power to pay back favors by shaping circumstances to strengthen the base of power.[22] As a soldier, I was careful to stay apolitical and always support the commander in chief at both the state and national level. As a result, I was very naïve about politics. Today I'm more sensitive to politically motivated tactics. I realize that politics is local, and can happen to men and women in all fields and walks of life every day. As a woman who believed in earning the rank, I also believed that elevating the Georgia Guard's standing in the nation would be rewarded. I took my work personally and had faith in the leadership to do the right thing. I don't think I'm alone. Women who find themselves in these politically driven situations often take it personally and look for answers when something doesn't make sense. It's our nature. But not everything in life makes sense. Superior qualifications and accomplishments don't always mean you'll get the promotion. In this case, I had no control over the governor's decision. The only thing I had control over was my response. All the while, I was still grieving the loss of my marriage, feeling the anger, hurt, and betrayal.

Once you realize that certain events are beyond your control, you can give yourself permission to move on. Every person's journey will be different, and you will have your share of dark days ahead. My marriage counselor gave me advice just a year earlier that I dusted off and used again for this devastating occurrence in my life. She told me to focus on my blessings in life and to make lemonade out of lemons. And that's what I did. I worked on strengthening my relationships with God, family, and friends. I searched my soul to start reinventing myself based on my PLP and True North. I had learned from my banking experience to be patient while searching for new opportunities. In other words, pick yourself up, dust yourself off, and start all over again. The strategy worked.

Exiting with Grace

When I left the meeting with the governor's chief of staff, I was calm. I didn't cry or get angry or show how upset I was. I didn't waste my breath saying anything petty or negative. I had already reminded the men in the room of what I had accomplished and what I was so proud to do for the organization. Getting upset wouldn't have made a difference in the outcome, but it would have made me look like I was either begging for them to keep me or asking for a fight—neither of which I wanted. As commander in chief of the Guard, the governor has the prerogative to appoint the generals he so desires to run it, and he had his own personal reasons for selecting the two individuals he did. In my heart, I knew I was the leader best suited for the job of the TAG due to my extensive training and performance. And yet, ultimately credentials did not matter.

I'm a mother. I have three daughters forging their own paths in life. I want them to see that I will always take the high ground—the right way to deal with tough circumstances. Regardless of what has happened to me thus far in my career, I have always made a point to carry myself in a professional manner, hold my head high, and be proud of my successes. My satisfaction is knowing that there are soldiers who still reach out to me to thank me for what I did for them years ago. They tell me how my tough love and leadership made them better individuals. I wanted those soldiers to be better because I wanted the organization to become stronger, and in the final moments of my career in the Guard, I stayed true to my values.

If It Bleeds, It Leads

In early 2012, I was proud to join the leadership team at a major state university in Georgia. But just a few weeks into my time there, I suddenly found myself in an awkward situation. A newspaper reporter had contacted me to ask about a U.S. Department of the Army Inspector General's (DAIG) complaint that had a series of allegations against me. I hadn't seen the complaint and was unaware that a complaint had even been filed, especially since I no longer wore the uniform. I asked the reporter to send me the complaint, so I could review it and provide my side of the story. He faxed it to me immediately. Sixteen allegations were outlined. *Sixteen.* Pages and pages of accusations citing examples of things I had allegedly done wrong or mishandled. The newspaper reporter told me it looked ugly, and that he wanted to hear my side but was under pressure from his editor to get it out fast. This gave me very little time to prepare for what would come next.

At that time a formal investigation hadn't even been started. Normally, the DAIG would call you to let you know you are the subject of an inquiry. Since that had not happened, it meant that the inspector general had not yet opened an investigation. The complaint is classified as "FOUO," or for official use only. The dissemination of the allegations is prohibited except as authorized in Army Regulation 20-1 and should not have been released outside of DAIG channels by the complainant. Yet a copy was sent to the governor's office. Then it was acquired by a reporter through an Open Records Act request, I suspect in an effort to justify my "replacement" as a general officer in the National Guard. Wanting to be transparent with my new employer and to not tarnish the university, I sought out the guidance and advice from a university public-affairs person. He went through each allegation with me, and was shocked at the lack of basis and contradictory wording of material in the report. He jokingly suggested that I write a book dedicating a chapter to each of the allegations and the twisted logic used to skew the justification.

The allegations accused me of having had an "inappropriate relationship" with my superior. My boss was a longtime mentor and someone I looked up to professionally, but there was never anything inappropriate between us. I was utterly offended and saddened by the accusations. The ironic thing is that as a woman trying to pave the way for other women to hold high-ranking positions in the Guard, I had worked hard to avoid the perception that there was anything inappropriate happening between me and any male superior I had worked with. Yes, we did travel together, much like the current generals in command now travel together. It's the nature of the work, and would not be an issue had I been a man. There was only one occasion when we accidentally had adjoining rooms, and I tried to have my room changed, but the hotel was fully booked and not able to change it. I even made a point of calling my then-husband, the only person I told, to let him know the situation and vent about how frustrated I was over it. So it was surprising for me to see this detail in the complaint. It also made me wonder if the complainant would automatically assume his wife was having an "inappropriate relationship" if accidentally assigned an adjoining room with her boss.

Another allegation in the complaint claimed that I was having an affair with one of my colonels, who had once, very publicly, given me flowers as a friendly gesture when he knew I was going through a rough time with my divorce. He had rescued the bouquet of assorted flowers from the trash after his daughter threw them (a gift from her ex-boyfriend) away, thinking they could be a bright spot in my day. It was a thoughtful gesture that I appreciated. He even took some ribbing from his fellow colonels who observed the act. The irony is that the last thing a man would do if he were having an affair with someone is to publicly present her with flowers.

I was beginning to build a solid reputation in the next phase of my career, having begun the process of reinventing myself in life after military service. Suddenly, unproven allegations by a vindictive former coworker cast a shadow over me. When the article was posted online, readers began anonymously posting comments. Some of the comments were very hurtful, and I was even called names, but I never engaged in the online discussion personally. It seemed demeaning to me to participate in something that felt so cowardly. I worked with the reporter to later have some of the comments redacted from the online discussion because they were untrue, egregious, and personal. It wasn't just the impact on my reputation and career that bothered me. I was more concerned about the impact on the reputation of the Georgia Army National Guard, an organization I had worked hard to professionalize over the last twenty years.

After a newspaper ran with the story, a local television station covered it as well. I became even more concerned about the impact on my family. My daughters were thirteen, twenty-two, and twenty-five at the time this was all happening. The youngest didn't really understand what was going on, but I had to explain to the older two what had happened, that the allegations were people's perceptions but not the reality, and that none of it was true. I reassured them that I loved their father (even though our relationship was rocky at the time) and that I loved them and would never do anything to compromise my role as a mother and wife. The entire situation was devastating.

As they say, if it bleeds, it leads, whether or not it is true. Ironically, the complainant, when pressed for evidence by the investigative news reporter, stated he "couldn't personally vouch for every allegation" he wrote, but that it "was a collaborative effort" with several other officers.[23] Interpretation: water-cooler rumors rolled together to look plausible. And that was the saddest, cruelest part for me.

Nine months after the story had been published, I was notified through proper channels of the allegations and a preliminary inquiry was opened by the DAIG. Within six months, the inquiry was completed, concluding the allegations in the complaint were unfounded and unsubstantiated. The victory felt hollow. The damage had been done.

The "Scarlet Letter Effect"

Reflecting on what happened, I feel that my being a woman made it easier for false accusations to be readily believed. It made it easy for me to be pushed aside by those who couldn't compete on a level playing field in terms of skills or competency. Your adversaries can take down your character—and then not have to compete against you based on merit—by spreading untrue allegations. Your reputation becomes tainted even if the allegations are never proven true. I refer to it as the "Scarlet Letter Effect," to play off the classic book *The Scarlet Letter*. In the story, set in 1600s Boston, a woman in the Puritan community is accused of adultery and forced to wear a scarlet-colored letter "A" as a sort of mark of her indiscretions for all to see.

My detractors, who had written these inspector-general complaints and filed anonymous letters, had created enough smoke to give the perception that there were doubts about my character, which could have provided the justification and "top cover" for my replacement. The real reason, if any, for my being let go would be overlooked due to the false scandal that had been created. They could say there was some concern about an improper relationship, and that I might have been promoted due to favoritism. I had an excellent track record on active duty and in the Georgia Army National Guard, earning early promotions to the next rank with minimal time in grade. But the allegations in the DAIG complaint, released to the media against DA policy, presumed me guilty before any investigation took place.

The Media: Judge, Jury, and Sometimes . . . Executioner

One thing I learned through the difficult moments in my career is that the media is a fair-weather companion. During good times in your career, your interactions with the media will be friendly and supportive. They may interview you for stories related to your area of expertise, cover events your organization is holding or sponsoring, etc. But when there's potentially something ugly on the horizon, true or not, the media defaults to getting the story out to its audience.

Oftentimes it comes down to the individual reporter and his or her sense of balance between truth and bleeding headlines. I recall two examples in my career when reporters took the time to sort through the details before writing the headline. One involved an allegation that I covered up a drug-use incident at a chaplain's training session because it involved the son of my administrative assistant. There was no substantiated drug use. The director of chaplains was on site and handled the situation professionally, transporting the ill soldier to the hospital for medical attention. The reporter dropped the story after realizing it had no merit. The second example involved a reporter who had gotten a scoop on perceived "favoritism" that resulted in me skirting deployment. The allegation claimed that I was removed from battalion command early to avoid being deployed in response to 9/11. I explained to the reporter that I transitioned out of a successful command in March 2001, six months prior to the horrific attacks on September 11, 2001. There was no way I would have known about a future attack, let alone a deployment of the battalion two years later. She realized the allegation was ludicrous and dropped the story.

Most who work in the media are conscientious and don't want to needlessly hurt people, destroy careers, or ruin lives. Unfortunately, they are in a competitive industry that expects results and operates under a constant sense of urgency to get a story on air, online, or in print before "the other guys." When I was let go from my position with the Georgia Army National Guard, there were a couple of reporters who wanted to interview me because they knew the situation didn't seem right. They knew I was the first female to be a general officer in the state, and one of the highest-ranking females in the state government. To just be dismissed like I was with no regard for what I had accomplished seemed "off." But I declined the interview invitations because I saw no utility in pointing out the obvious and getting drawn into a blame game and mudslinging.

As much as I wanted to defend my honor and integrity, I had to consider the potential consequences of firing back. My mom's advice about not wrestling with pigs because you'll both get dirty also weighed in on my decision-making process. What will be gained or lost in the long term by my immediate response? My answer to that question drove me to this conclusion: I must survive this battle to stay in the fight. People are going to believe what they want to believe, but for those who really know you and know what you've done, you don't hide, you don't recoil, and you don't allow yourself to be pulled into the rumors and to disparage the leadership. The change of leadership was already traumatic for the organization, and I didn't want it to get further tarnished with internal politics.

The way the media operates—rushing to be the first organization to run a story—can sometimes mean that innocent, hardworking professionals become the subject of public scrutiny. This happens when a story that hasn't been fully researched or evaluated and contains false information is released. If you become the subject of a story the media is interested in, here are some tips:

- Be polite to the reporter, even if you feel like your integrity is being questioned.
- Try to remember that they're ultimately just doing their job.
- Stay calm and don't give them a reason to make you the subject of further scrutiny.
- Ask them as much as you can to find out what they know.
  o How and from whom are they getting their information?
  o Have they found two other sources to back up the information they have obtained from a single source?
  o When are they planning to run the story they are working on?
  o Can you get a draft before the story is released?
  o Are they contacting opposing sides to ensure a balanced story?
  o How much time do you have to gather your thoughts before they need a statement from you?

If you already have a lawyer or public-relations person assisting you, be sure to tell the reporter you want that person to be with you or on the call when you are being interviewed. Remember, you have the right to decline being interviewed, but keep in mind that sometimes declining to be interviewed, or having no comment, can be seen as an "admission of guilt" if spun a certain way by the media.

I strongly recommend engaging the help of a public-relations professional when possible, as I did when the story of the DAIG report was breaking. A PR professional will help you sort through all the "noise" around the incident and focus on the important things for you to say when being interviewed. They also may be able to find "holes" in how the media plans to report a story, and give you suggestions on specific things to say to the media to try to request more balanced coverage. Words matter. For example, I pointed out to a reporter that he was creating a bias by describing the lunches I went to with my boss as "lunch dates" versus what they really were, "lunch meetings." He still went with "lunch dates."

When They Go Low, I Go High

Where can I even begin? I learned a great deal during these difficult professional and personal times in my life. I already knew who I was as a person and what I really believed in, but going through these experiences with losing my job, having my reputation questioned, watching my twenty-six-year marriage disintegrate, really reinforced for me that no matter how difficult things got, I could still move in the direction of my True North and stay on course in my life's journey.

Think through the consequences of everything you do. This message is especially for women: no matter what level of accomplishment you achieve, you're always on duty, watched under a microscope by superiors, peers, media, and the court of public opinion. We often don't think about these things until we're in a bad situation. It can be exhausting to always be on guard, but you've got to be your own best protector. Even if your boss says, "Don't worry about it. It's not a problem"—no, it *is* a problem. Help him understand it's not about him, it's about others' perceptions. Guard your professional and personal reputation as much as you possibly can, even though, in a perfect world, you shouldn't have to.

One needs to have a tough skin and even stronger core values. I don't have a magical solution or a quick fix for steeling your resolve, but I can tell you it's critical to being a leader who experiences moments of real struggle in their career. There will always be people out there who will want to see you falter to help advance their own goals. You must not take things personally or internalize the anger and pain. It will weigh you down and keep you from staying in the fight and moving on to success somewhere else. Stay on the high ground, keep your head held high, and move on to where your skill set will be appreciated and where you can make a difference.

Compass Check: Forging Ahead

What adversity have you faced so far in your career? Whether big or small, every issue you've encountered has helped shape you into the professional you are today, for better or worse. Have you been let go from a job? Accused of something you didn't do? Made major mistakes? While you may face obstacles that seem insurmountable, keep your sights set on what is important to you and life will fall into place. If you can forge ahead in the face of adversity to work toward your purpose in life, you are a leader, leading yourself through life's journey.

Success is not final, failure is not fatal: it is the
courage to continue that counts.

—Winston Churchill

IX

BRING IT ON

Surviving and Thriving through It All

Looking back on the challenges of my career, I have realized that I was naïve and completely unprepared for the politics that surrounded each position. Every organization and each career path possesses some degree of politics. Normally, the higher you progress and the more visibility you have in an organization, the more likely you are to face "office politics." Behind-the-scenes, personal motivations can impact what positions are kept or eliminated, who is selected to fill or be removed from a position, what the salary level should be, and so much more. Unfortunately, being the most qualified at something isn't enough anymore. There are any number of reasons for politics, and they will have nothing to do with how well you are at performing in the actual job. More often than not it comes down to who you know, or more importantly, who knows you.

We all will face struggles in both our personal and professional lives, and when those things happen it's natural to be angry and negative. But it's important to handle yourself with dignity and professionalism to prevent further complications. Give yourself the first few moments to process the information and vent internally, then shift your mental energy to focusing on a course of action.

First, accept that there is an issue. Take a deep, cleansing breath and wrap your mind around what has happened. Work to understand what you are feeling. Label the emotions so you can later make sure you are processing through each of them and not fixating on them to your detriment. Identify the exact issue without the peripheral drama. Even though you may not be able to influence it, try to clarify what has caused the problem you are now facing. Often, clarifying the cause of the issue allows you to not blame yourself. Next, you will need to find the courage to take action. Action can come in many forms, to include deciding not to do anything at all. Is there someone you can report the problem to or discuss it with? If there is a manager or leader you can speak to, present the facts. Be calm and straightforward and tell it like it is. It will take courage to speak out for yourself, but if you chose to be a leader, you must learn to act quickly in the most difficult of situations. I was once at a conference where women shared stories of their struggle in higher education. One woman told her story of constant scrutiny as a member of the LGBTQ community and was so emotional that she broke down in tears. We all shared her pain, having been judged for one reason or another. It took real courage for her to share something so personal and to fight the feeling of vulnerability with which she was coping.

It has taken a great deal of courage for me to go through the process of writing this book—dredging up painful memories and experiences and reliving the emotions I felt with each phase of my life. Looking back, there are some instances where I think that maybe I should have done things differently. Maybe I should have better prepared myself for the politics I would face, and learned to engage in it. But you know what they say about hindsight, it's 20/20! Besides, that wasn't me. My hope in sharing these stories and advice is that you will learn to not just move past difficult experiences and hurdles in your career and personal life, but to come away from them a more effective and powerful leader.

Give It Back Shinier . . .

I have achieved many things in my career paths that didn't advance me personally, but made the organization I was with better. As a servant leader, my focus has always been to improve the organization, not to toot my own horn. If I was constantly worried about my ego and making myself look good, I wouldn't be truly focused on the mission at hand. Whether it was my rank in the Georgia Army National Guard or my civilian role with a state university, I have always strived to bring respect and credibility to the organizations and people for whom I worked.

One of my mentors, Brigadier General Terrell Reddick, told me once that when you get promoted, you borrow the rank, make the organization better, and then give it back. Don't let your ego get attached to your title or rank. It's not about you, but the legacy that you leave. The goal of a leader should always be to leave things better than they were when you started, even if in the end you leave the organization on difficult terms. The professionals in any organization will recognize your authenticity and appreciate what you have done for them and their mission. Let your inspiration be fed from their positive energy and sincere smiles of thanks. Compartmentalize the naysayers and people with self-serving agendas. They are beneath you and should never be allowed to define your character or integrity, because they have little. Surround yourself with positive people who will lift you up and help you move to the next chapter in your life.

Blindsided

When you begin a new job, it can be easy to get attached to a fancy job title or big salary. Don't be lured in. Don't get attached to the job title; get attached to the job. You have to love going to work every morning, but also be prepared to be blindsided at any moment. An organization can "break up" with you. Don't build your entire identity and self-worth around your job title, because there is so much more to you than just a title.

Do you have an exit strategy in mind for if or when you lose or leave your current job? If not, start brainstorming! I made the mistake of being unprepared for the next phase of my career when I was serving in the Georgia Army National Guard. I had given twenty years of my life to the Georgia Guard and it had become my family, for better or for worse. I was honored to serve among so many patriotic men and women. I had put my heart and soul into being the best leader I could for such a worthy group of soldiers. I hadn't given much thought to what I would do if I wasn't serving the organization. When I was given the replacement notice and had only a couple weeks left, I immediately regretted not having an exit strategy. I was so immersed in doing my job that I didn't take the time to look out for myself and my family.

Even if you feel secure in your job, always be thinking a few moves ahead. A sudden retirement or resignation of a top leader can throw your world into a tailspin with little warning. Think about what other type of work you might enjoy and other places you may like to work. What skills or qualifications do you possess, and how can you rebrand and then market yourself? Are there skill sets you should enhance or certifications to add to your tool kit, especially when it comes to the use of technology? Where should you be networking to create a safety net in the event you do need to move on? I can't overemphasize this next point: it's more about who knows you than who you know. Network and build relationship inside and outside the workplace. Take credit for your successes and offer to share your insights. People will remember you if they can associate your name with adding value to their business. Take the time to help yourself now, because in the end, you will be your own best career manager.

Keep Getting Up after You're Knocked Down

No matter how many times you get knocked down in life, it's still a traumatic and hurtful experience each time, especially when your character is wrongfully besmirched. Through all of my life hurdles, I have never given up, and neither should you. Here's my silver lining—I can share with you that after each difficult experience I have endured, I have gotten better at knowing myself and understanding my feelings and responses. I'm more predictable in my processing because I've been hurt and betrayed a number of times and I recognize the pain. As mentioned in the first tenant of my PLP in chapter II, I live my life by the Warrior Ethos: I always place the mission first, I never accept defeat, I never quit, and I never leave a fallen comrade. Starting with my experiences at West Point, I have gained the confidence that no matter what, I will live my life by this ethos. When you face a sudden change in life, it will hurt. You may even think yourself a failure. But if you learn from the setback and grow stronger, chalk the setback up as a success. Give yourself time to process the grief before forcing your mind to move on, then spend your mental energy on the next chapter in your life.

Every person's life journey is unique. For me, I have used my speed bumps in life as an opportunity to rebrand myself and reevaluate how I can better align with my True North. I have had to dig deep and drum up the courage to start over. It's not easy, but when measured against the options of quitting or accepting defeat, I've chosen to drive on. I've had a few false starts, especially with my banking job, but I learned to be patient and do some soul-searching before jumping into the first opportunity offered. If you had told me twenty years ago that I would have worked for a major university following my time in the military, I'm not sure I would have believed you. But when the opportunity presented itself, I reflected and realized that I possessed a skill set that was transferable and leadership that was valued. I respected my immediate supervisor and the president of the university. These were two men who had servant-leader hearts and values that were aligned with my own. The combination of trusted leaders and my own proven record gave me the courage to rise up to the challenge and continue my life's journey.

Pay It Forward in a New Way

As your work environment and family situation change, so will your focus when it comes to your interests and volunteer work. Your time is a valuable resource, so take a moment to analyze why you're contributing in certain areas and if they are aligned with your PLP. Each time you enter into something new—whether it be a new town you have moved to, a new company you work for, or a new group of people you've befriended—look for ways to best serve in that new community. It's okay to be a bystander initially and to get your bearings, but once you start to sense opportunities, go for it.

It is important to me to be viewed as a resource and an asset in my community and organization. As I reflect on leaders who impressed me as sincere and genuine, I realize they always did more than their job description. They walked the talk, and became a part of the solution by volunteering in schools, churches, and civic groups—all of which made a difference. That strong sense of "caring" has driven me to get involved.

Our men and women currently in the service and those veterans who have proudly served our nation will always have a special place in my heart, even though I myself no longer wear the uniform. I choose to stay connected in a variety of ways. When I recently moved to the North Georgia mountains, I reached out to a hospice group and went through orientation and training to visit veterans in hospice care. I was honored to hold the hand of a WWII veteran who told me about his service under General George Patton, and that he attended a church service with Patton the week before he was killed. It was an awesome and unexpected experience that I will always cherish.

Desiring to stay within the education system, I sought out opportunities to meet educators by attending the county's monthly board of education meetings. I reached out to the local technical college and asked if I could attend their board of directors' monthly meeting. Each meeting created more opportunities to know the movers and shakers, as well as the front-burner issues of each organization. Being prepared with a short elevator speech and then following up with an email proved to be an effective way to set up meetings to go into more detail and offer my services.

I continue to speak publicly at events and advocate for our service members and the military. It's been my honor for almost a decade to volunteer time to screen admission packets and interview applicants to West Point seeking a nomination from Senator Johnny Isakson. Personally interacting with over thirty interviewees each year renews my faith in our next generation to lead this nation. For the last four years, I have also been on the advisory board for the Shepherd Center in Atlanta, specializing in rehabilitation for people with spinal cord injury, brain injury, multiple sclerosis, and the SHARE Initiative to support injured military members. Georgia Guard soldiers have found new life thanks to the vision of the Shepherd family. I am also an advisor to Warrior2Citizen, a nonprofit that helps service members and veterans cope with the impact of trauma and ease the transition back into life as a private citizen after serving in the military. I've dedicated time to assist Georgia State University with their research on moral injury and its impact on both male and female soldiers. I accepted the challenge to found and preside over Georgia's first chapter of Women in Defense, a nonprofit supporting women in all sectors of the defense industry. Inspired by the mission of Women Veterans Social Justice, I worked with the group's leadership to help heal the wounds of female soldiers who had been the victim of sexual assault. It was a heartbreaking and humbling experience.

I don't know what tomorrow's opportunities hold, but I can share that my volunteer work is, and will continue to be, in line with my mission as a servant leader to help others find their way, especially our military members and women. Take a moment to think about what you have to offer. Have you felt called to volunteer somewhere, but then talked yourself out of it? Start with a small-time commitment on a temporary basis, and you'll soon find out how rewarding your service can be. While you're paying it forward, you'll receive the side benefits of networking and growing your leadership potential in a nonthreatening environment, pushing you closer to achieving your True North.

Force Yourself into a New Perspective

If you enter a new industry or field at some point during your career, you may realize that it's important to understand the core basics of the business model of your organization. Understanding what the organization produces or offers will help you better see how you can improve or enhance the organization.

While working in the administration at the university, it was very rare that I got the opportunity to see what things were like from a classroom perspective. My boss at the time challenged me to put myself in the shoes of the faculty to see what kinds of challenges and issues they deal with in their roles. I met with several of the deans to find the best fit for my experiences, and I was delighted to be invited as a guest lecturer of leadership for the Executive Masters in Business Administration (EMBA) Program. The lecture was broken up into two two-hour sessions and was promoted as being presented by a true practitioner of leadership—someone who has "been there, done that"—rather than a theoretical teacher of leadership. My lecture added value to the Capstone Leadership course and provided an exciting chance for me to share leadership lessons that I have developed over my career.

That's not to say I wasn't a bit nervous at first, as I felt out of my element at the front of an amphitheater-style classroom facing thirty-five graduate students, but I quickly grew comfortable in the role. Instructing the students in leadership skills was another way to pay it forward, another way to help others who might someday find themselves in positions similar to what I've experienced in my life and career. It was validation, in a sense, that the practices I had developed up to that point in my career to grow my own leadership abilities could be effectively used by others. It also gave me a clearer picture of what it was like to be part of the university's faculty, collaborating with the dean and fellow professors to reinforce their material with the students while introducing concepts to support the student textbook. I had to learn the teaching platforms and how to use the classroom technology, an area that was totally foreign to me as an administrator.

The professor role gave me great context for my primary responsibilities as an administrator developing new policies and procedures. I was a better leader for having learned the core mission of the organization firsthand. My experience with the EMBA course remains one of my highlights with the university, and I look forward to future opportunities to lecture leaders of tomorrow on leadership. I encourage you to stretch past your comfort zone with new roles, for it is through stretching that you can experience true growth and unexpected fulfillment.

Compass Check: Are You Ready to Move past Failure?

What can you do if you suffer a career or personal pitfall? It goes without saying that you should learn from your mistakes and not make the same errors in the future. But don't just avoid making the same mistakes. Grow, change, and become stronger than ever. You'll get tired, you'll get knocked down, and it will hurt like hell, but you need to get back on your feet. If you haven't identified your True North and your PLP, it's time to get started. Lean on your support system of family, friends, and mentors to help rejuvenate your confidence and remind you of what is most important to you in life.

What else do you have to contribute to an industry? What other talents or skills do you have that you should be sharing with the world? What areas do you need to improve on? Be brave and ask former colleagues and staff for feedback on your leadership style and practices. This will not be easy. No one likes to admit that they are not perfect and have areas where they need to improve. But if you've experienced a big roadblock in your career, it's now the best time to evaluate and shift directions. Keep networking, think strategically, and find people who can help you grow and change.

If you are a woman, be prepared to prove yourself in every new role. This will be exhausting, and may chip away at your motivation, but go into each situation with your eyes open. More often than not, you will have to work harder than you ever imagined to make an impact, but you have no choice if you desire to keep advancing and growing as a leader. I have spent much of my career cracking the glass ceiling for the women who will come after me, and I plan to keep doing so regardless of how many times I get knocked down.

No matter where you are in your life and career, through identifying your True North and staying true to your life's path, you, too, can successfully navigate the climb. Drive on!

Appendix

Maria's Personal Leadership Philosophy (PLP)

Tried and tested for the last thirty years!

1. **Live by the Warrior Ethos.**
   I will always place the mission first.
   I will never accept defeat.
   I will never quit.
   I will never leave a fallen comrade.

2. **Follow the Golden Rule.**
   Treat others as I would expect to be treated. Punish bad behavior privately, offer praise in public, and no matter what, always respect the person.

3. **Give back through servant leadership.**
   I have learned that it is a greater gift to give than to receive. I exist to serve others and to work toward the greater good, not toward my own personal gain.

4. **Live peacefully by developing mind, body, and soul.**
   I strive to live an integrated life, developing my mind, body, and soul. I give my mind time to think and reflect, and I work to stay informed. Exercise and diet are important to my mental and physical health, but I work hardest to feed my soul with faith, prayer, and love of family and friends. If I neglect any one of these three tenets, I feel out of balance with myself.

5. **Laugh as often as possible.**
   I try to laugh as often as I can, especially at myself. I keep a sense of humor and humility, knowing I'm not in control. I can't be a perfectionist and ever be happy!

Maria's Leadership Credo

To effectively lead, I must:

- Be with people who want to excel and achieve something in life
- Set standards and communicate
- Teach to achieve the standard; require all to excel
- Do not offer or accept excuses; there aren't any good ones
- Build self-image/confidence
- Challenge employees; they expect it

How I see my role:

- Build teams and lead teams
- Set priorities
- Focus on the future: strategic and operational perspective
- Encourage risk-taking and learning
- Mentor, coach, and teach

My style and leadership preferences:

- I expect options when you bring me a problem.
- I don't micromanage; I will provide guidance.
- I trust you to do your job to the best of your ability (if you need training, I'll help you get it; if you don't want to work here, I'll help you find another job).

- I demand the Four Cs: candor, commitment, courage, and caring.
- I expect you to be big enough to admit mistakes.
- I value each *contributing* member of our team for the differences you bring.
- I view bad-mouthing, backstabbing, and petty attitudes as disruptive to the team, and will work to eradicate such behavior.
- I view a half-truth as a whole lie; be straight up with me.
- I believe professional bearing and appearance is important. Always look professional; it's a sign of commitment, and it tells your story.
- My door is open.

SAMPLE MEETING AGENDA

When meeting with a committee or team, it is important to maximize the time you have together to accomplish your goals. I have found that having a very organized agenda is important in keeping everyone focused. Below is a sample meeting agenda.

Meeting Agenda

Date: July 14, 2020
Time: 10:00–11:30 a.m.
Location: Campus Hall 1234
Project/Meeting Name: Sexual Assault–Warning Notification Program

Item No.	Topic	Facilitator	Time
1.	**Welcome** • Purpose: Create a unified approach in general sexual-assault warnings • Deliverable: Sexual Assault–Warning Notification Policy content and procedures • Ground Rules: Guarding of confidential information; respectful listening • Introductions: Attendees	Committee Leader	5 min.
2.	**Discuss Recent Incident** • Determination to send out sexual-assault warning • Recipients: students, faculty, and staff • Best practices in generating warning	Public Safety Director	15 min.

3.	**Warning-Notice Content** • Review template for warning notice • Recommendations for edits from attendees	Committee Leader	30 min.
4.	**External Communications** • Follow up on messages to campus community and beyond	Public Relations	15 min.
5.	**Looking Ahead** • Reviews following each incident • Collaboration with other campus departments o Victims Advocate Office o Student Affairs o Office of Safety and Health o Legal Affairs o Others? • Best practices • Future training	Committee Leader and all	15 min.
6.	**Closing** • Alibi fire? • Confirm action items/next steps	Committee Leader	10 min.

BLANK TEMPLATE: CAREER-PROGRESSION PLANNING TOOL

Career-progression planning is a process of managing the staff and positions in the organization. A team of trustworthy leaders from your organization will assemble as a board to plan ahead for the staffin g in the organization. Here is a blank career-progression planning tool for you to use for your organization.

Future Positions:	Future Positions:	Future Positions:
_____	_____	_____
_____	_____	_____
_____	_____	_____

Name:	Name:	Name:
Position:	Position:	Position:
Date Assigned:	Date Assigned:	Date Assigned:

Possible Replacements:	Possible Replacements:	Possible Replacements:
_____	_____	_____
_____	_____	_____
_____	_____	_____

CRITICAL–INFORMATION MATRIX (CIM)

A big subcomponent of managing time is prioritizing the flow of information in an organization. A Critical-Information Matrix (CIM) can provide insight for you and your team in what you want to hear and when you want to hear it. The first step is to outline the roles/positions in your organization that need to be notified of important events or information, and then break them up into groups. Here is an example:

Notification Positions/Roles	Groups				
	A	B	C	D	E
President (CEO)	●				
Chief Business Officer (CBO)	●	●			
Facility Management Officer (FMO)		●			
Safety and Security Officer		●			
Chief Legal Counsel			●		
Human Resources Officer (HRO)			●		
Public Information Officer (PIO)				●	
Chief Information Officer (CIO)					●

Next, outline the types of events, emergencies, etc. that would be potential issues for your organization and deemed critical information to share. The following sample CIM is meant to illustrate what a completed one will look like. In the CIM you will list out:

- The type of information (assign each an ID number)
- How quickly notification of the information must happen
- What group(s) needs to be notified

ID Number	Description	Notification	Group
01	Information on a potential dangerous incident, safety risk, or other event that could affect the organization	Immediate	A, B, D
02	Death, severe illness, or injury of staff or contract employee	Immediate	B, C, D
03	Reports of or actual active shooter at facility	Immediate	A, B, C, D
04	Personal attack, discrimination, or bullying involving employees	Next day	C
05	Major damage to the facility of the organization (flooding, storm damage, fire, collapse, etc.)	Immediate	A, B, D
06	Critical issues with technology or power (power loss, server crash, alarm system)	Within 12 hours	A, B, E
07	Sensitive item is compromised or lost (keys, access cards, weapons)	Within 12 hours	A, B, plus possible others

ID Number	Description	Notification	Group
08	Sensitive data is lost or compromised (customer information, passwords, payment information, etc.)	Immediate or case-dependent but within 8 hours	A, D, E
09	Financial discrepancies, accounting concerns, or theft	Next day	A, C
10	Potential visit of inspectors, corporate officers, ranking/measurement agencies	Within 12 hours	A, B
11	Media coverage of the organization or its staff (positive and negative, actual or anticipated)	Immediate	A, D
12	Staffing issue that could impact the organization's ability to function or provide a service	Within 12 hours	A, B, C, D
13	Pandemic or infectious-disease cases that may impact staffing or safety	Immediate	A, B, C, D

Notes and Tips

At times there may be additions to groups identified above based on the incident.

I used letters to create notification groups instead of numbers. Why? Because I found out early on that everyone wants to be number one, and you can't be effective in your notification system if the entire team is in group number one!

ACKNOWLEDGMENTS

I have been blessed to serve with many of America's finest men and women in the service of our nation. Soldiers from all walks of life, brought together by a common purpose: to defend the constitution of the United States against all enemies, foreign and domestic. I served with many notable soldiers, especially those who are the backbone of the U.S. Army, the noncommissioned officers (NCOs). From platoon sergeants to command sergeants major, I have valued their wise counsel and leadership provided for over thirty years. Of all the noncommissioned officers I have worked with, Command Sergeant Major James Nelson was the epitome of the NCO corps. Thank you, James, for your unwavering support and course corrections when I needed them.

There were many commissioned officers who grounded me as a junior officer on active duty. At Fort Hood, Texas, Captain Timothy Lamb taught me to trust my gut and Captain Dick Wong introduced me to the bigger picture in life. Lieutenant Colonels "Dutch" Holland and Ted Stafford encouraged me to compete for jobs women had not yet held at Fort McPherson, Georgia. Colonel Gerald Lord gave me the opportunity and mentored me through the dual-hat position of being Fort Mac's first female military police company commander, as well as Forces Command's commander of troops for ceremonies. I thank them for their confidence in me.

Continuing my service as a Georgia Guardsman, I was fortunate to have three primary mentors. Brigadier General Tom McCullough helped me keep things in perspective and always led by doing the right thing for the right reason. He paved the way for a more professional organization by not tolerating prejudice and bias within the ranks. Thank you, sir, for your steadfast integrity and willingness to do the harder right. Brigadier General Terrell Reddick had a subtle yet powerful way of letting you know what he expected. He always put the soldier first, keeping the staff and leaders focused on what mattered most. He coined the phrase "Soldiers Matter," and I knew what it meant. Cancer stole this great leader from us too soon. His passion for soldiers left an indelible mark on me. Throughout my Guard service, Major General William T. Nesbitt has been the most impactful of my mentors. He leveled the playing field many times so I could compete for roles of greater responsibility. He provided support and encouragement along the way, allowing me to learn from my mistakes and grow into a strategic leader. I am proud to have served under his leadership and to now call him my friend. Thank you, sir, for your moral courage and perseverance to stay on the high ground.

After exchanging my military uniform for a business suit and high heels, I had the good fortune to work in higher education as the deputy for Colonel (retired) Randy Hinds, a thirty-year U.S. Army veteran. Randy made the transition to civilian life easier with his many mentoring sessions, shared war stories, and perspectives on organizational people and processes. He encouraged me to meet with key leaders, attend meetings outside of our department, and get into the classroom to better understand the needs of faculty and students. Together, our divergent styles complemented each other, focusing the operations of the university on what mattered most, the students. Randy, thank you for your mentorship, your friendship, and especially for taking a chance on me.

Successfully navigating leadership at the senior levels requires having subordinates who will have the courage to speak truth to power. I made a concerted effort to not surround myself with "yes-men," but with those who had diversity of thought and experiences. It has brought me great satisfaction to see the majority of those I considered mentees to have risen through the ranks. Colonel Peter VanAmburgh reminded me that setbacks were merely part of life's "hardening process." Colonel Keith Knowlton helped me to strengthen my commander's message. Colonel Lee Durham sharpened my debate skills with his lawyer prowess, and more importantly, commanded the 48th Infantry Brigade during a challenging tour of duty in Afghanistan. I could always count on Colonel Brent Bracewell to be the positive and uplifting leader in the room, willing to add value with his aviator perspective. And Colonel Matt Smith, a brilliant leader with a sarcastic wit who taught me tactical patience. My appreciation and admiration go out to the colonels I worked with who are now generals: Tom Blackstock for the tremendous effort modernizing the Georgia Guard's infrastructure and his steadfast support; Reggie Neal for stepping up and working harder to break down further barriers and lead our soldiers well; Randall Simmons for trusting my Plan B in his career development to better serve our soldiers; John King for giving me clarity in the tough times with a twist of humor; and Tom Carden for his straight talk and numerous "Cardenisms," some used in this book.

This project got its start over lunch several years ago with a good friend and mentor, Jane Goldner, who has had a distinguished career as a consultant, role integration coach, national speaker, and author. Jane and I met over twenty years ago when she was part of a consulting team to reorganize the Georgia Guard, and we stayed in touch over the years, sharing our stories and venting with each other. Jane, thank you for the nudge and advice that got me here today.

Once I decided to embark on this journey, I reached out to other authors for their advice. Jeffrey Tobias Halter, author of *Why Women: The Leadership Imperative to Advancing Women and Engaging Men*, shared his experiences in organizing the material and encouraged me not to get discouraged while writing the book. Erin Wolf gave me a copy of her book, *Lessons from the Trenches: A Woman's Guide to Winning the Corporate Game*, reminding me she had used two of my stories in her book and now it was my time. Eddie Williams, a military colleague and friend, inspired me with his moving story told in the book *Son of a Soldier*. Phyllis Newhouse and I participated on a panel together at the 2014 Women Veterans Social Justice conference and became instant friends, swapping stories of our Army experiences. A successful entrepreneur as founder of Xtreme Solutions Inc., Phyllis gave me an invaluable opportunity to present my story to multimillionaire women CEOs at the Women Presidents' Organization meeting in Montreal, gaining insightful feedback that helped me shape this book. Phyllis inspired me with her uplifting story as the contributing author of Chapter 28: Know Your Reason Why in the book *We Got Mojo!: Stories of Inspiration and Perspiration* by lead author Dr. Raul A. Deju.

I couldn't have completed this book without the expert advice, shepherding, and encouragement of the team at BookLogix. After meeting them, I knew my book would be in good hands. Their shared enthusiasm for my story kept me heartened through the numerous manuscript edits and brainstorming sessions. The creative thinkers at BookLogix led me through the four-year process and were terrific to work with the entire time. I thank each of you.

I had always wondered what it would be like to work with women, having spent the majority of my adult life in a male-dominated environment. I got the answer during my tenure in higher education, and what a wonderful experience it was. Dawn Gamadanis, Laura McMillan, Kathy Maschke, and Teen Lowery created a synergy that made every day impactful. Their enthusiasm for this project kept me moving forward, even after my departure from the university. We trusted and motivated each other during times of personal and professional hardships, continuing our friendship even as we travel on different trajectories in life. I am blessed that our paths have crossed, and I will always cherish our friendship.

As I rebranded for the third time, searching for a purposeful mission and a boss I could work for and respect, Chaplain and Superintendent Charles Wayne Lovell entered my life's journey. His powerful vision to better serve the wounded and at-risk students of North Georgia through the Mountain Education Charter High School captivated my soul. Wayne challenged me to lead him and his leaders through an intense strategic thinking and planning process that focused Mountain Ed on its core mission of giving students a second chance to earn a high school diploma. Thank you, Dr. Lovell, for your servant leader's heart and for inspiring me to serve once again.

I could never have completed this book without the love of my family. My sister, Eva Mendsen, and my brother, Navy Commander Dr. Anthony Corsini, both cheered me on throughout the project. Go Army, beat Navy! My supportive parents, Anthony and Dolores Corsini, both teachers for three decades, provided comic relief during my times of writer's block. My father took on the arduous role of editor-in-chief, spending hours reshaping several chapters and strengthening my delivery as only a father who has had a front-row seat to my life's journey could do. Thank you, Mom and Dad, for your love, encouragement, and patience, and for seeing me through thick and thin, including this marathon project.

Finally, my daughters, Ava Stuck, Chelsea Britt (soon to be Dennison), and Joy Britt. They are my inspiration for writing this book. As young women juggling many roles already, this book will help them to appreciate why Mom was stressed out from time to time. It is my prayer that by sharing my hard knocks, they will be better prepared and strengthened for their own journey. Thank you, girls, for your sacrifices over the years. They have not gone unnoticed. Please know that of all the roles I have had the honor to serve in, being your mother has made me the proudest. I love you.

NOTES

1. DeWolf, Mark. "12 Stats About Working Women." U.S. Department of Labor Blog. March 1, 2017. https://blog.dol.gov/2017/03/01/12-stats-about-working-women.
2. Zarya, Valentina. "The Percentage of Female CEOs in the Fortune 500 Drops to 4%." *Fortune*. June 6, 2016. http://fortune.com/2016/06/06/women-ceos-fortune-500-2016/.
3. Zwirn, Ed. "Leaning In: Women in Finance." CFO. May 04, 2016. http://ww2.cfo.com/people/2016/05/leaning-in-women-in-finance/.
4. Brooks, Rebecca Beatrice. "Deborah Sampson: Woman Warrior of the American Revolution." History of Massachusetts. December 29, 2011. http://historyofmassachusetts.org/deborah-sampson-woman-warrior-of-the-american-revoultion/.
5. Grimm, Robert, Jr., Kimberly Spring, and Nathan Dietz. "The Health Benefits of Volunteering: A Review of Recent Research." Corporation for National Community Service. April 2007. http://www.nationalservice.gov/pdf/07_0506_hbr.pdf.
6. Wilson, Julie. "New Study Proves Exposure to Nature Directly Improves Happiness." Natural News. January 15, 2014. http://www.naturalnews.com/043518_happiness_nature_mental_health.html.
7. Shah, Yagana. "New Study Proves That Laughter Really Is the Best Medicine." *The Huffington Post*. April 22, 2014. http://www.huffingtonpost.com/2014/04/22/laughter-and-memory_n_5192086.html.
8. "Alice's Adventures in Wonderland." *Alice's Adventures in Wonderland*, by Lewis Carroll. http://www.gutenberg.org/files/11/11-h/11-h.htm.
9. Harari, Oren. *The Leadership Secrets of Colin Powell*. Collingdale, PA: Diane Publishing Co., 2004. Page 168.
10. "Bluebird CEO: You Can't Manage a Secret." My AJC.

http://www.myajc.com/news/business/blue-bird-ceo-you-cant-manage-a-secret/nb2d4/.

11. Japanese Proverb Quotes. Quoteland. Quotations by Author. http://www.quoteland.com/author/Japanese-Proverb-Quotes/105/.

12. Walton, Sam, and John Huey. *Sam Walton, Made in America: My Story*. New York: Bantam Books Trade Paperbacks, 2012.

13. Collins, Jim. *Good to Great: Why Some Companies Make the Leap . . . and Others Don't*. London: Random House, 2001.

14. Covey, Stephen, A. Roger Merrill, and Rebecca R. Merrill. *First Things First*. New York: Simon & Schuster, 2017.

15. Fallon, Nicole. "35 Inspiring Leadership Quotes." Business News Daily. September 9, 2015. http://www.businessnewsdaily.com/7481-leadership-quotes.html.

16. "Arthur Ashe Quotes." BrainyQuote. https://www.brainyquote.com/quotes/quotes/a/arthurashe371528.html?src=t_destination.

17. Rothwell, J. Dan. *In Mixed Company: Communicating in Small Groups and Teams*. Boston, MA: Cengage Learning, 2016. Page 421.

18. "George Patton Quotes." Wisdom of the Wise. http://www.wisdom-of-the-wise.com/George-Patton.htm.

19. Nelson, Audrey. "Are Women Queen Bees?" *Psychology Today*. October 01, 2016. https://www.psychologytoday.com/blog/he-speaks-she-speaks/201610/are-women-queen-bees.

20. "Rewards Quotes." BrainyQuote. http://www.brainyquote.com/quotes/keywords/rewards.html.

21. Groth, Aimee. "Sheryl Sandberg: 'The Most Important Career Choice You'll Make Is Who You Marry.'" *Business Insider*. December 1, 2011. http://www.businessinsider.com/sheryl-sandberg-career-advice-to-women-2011-12.

22. Salzer, James. "Deal fills top jobs with insiders." *The Atlanta Journal-Constitution*. November 6, 2011. https://www.ajc.com/news/local/deal-fills-top-jobs-with-insiders/7fe8cBy3Vu76bRD6ntPqmN/.

23. Galloway, Jim. "Two Guard Generals Accused of 'Improper' Relationship." *The Atlanta Journal-Constitution*. March 8, 2012.

CPSIA information can be obtained
at www.ICGtesting.com
Printed in the USA
LVHW110708101119
636864LV00008B/26/P